GOLD RUSH

GOLD RUSH

What It Takes to Win Olympic Greatness

Michael Johnson

GOLD RUSH

What Makes an Olympic Champion?

Michael Johnson

HarperSport

An Imprint of HarperCollins*Publishers*

First published in 2011 by
HarperSport
an imprint of HarperCollins*Publish*
77–85 Fulham Palace Road,
Hammersmith, London W6 8JB

www.harpercollins.co.uk

10 9 8 7 6 5 4 3 2 1

© Michael Johnson 2011

Michael Johnson asserts the moral right to be
identified as the author of this work

A catalogue record of this book is
available from the British Library

Photographs courtesy of the author
except where stated otherwise

ISBN 978-0-00-741191-7 (hardback)
ISBN 978-0-00-741192-4 (trade paperback)

Printed and bound in Great Britain by
Clays Ltd, St Ives plc

MIX
Paper from
responsible sources
FSC **FSC™ C007454**
www.fsc.org

FSC™ is a non-profit international organisation established to promote
the responsible management of the world's forests. Products carrying the
FSC label are independently certified to assure customers that they come
from forests that are managed to meet the social, economic and
ecological needs of present and future generations,
and other controlled sources.

Find out more about HarperCollins and the environment at
www.harpercollins.co.uk/green

To my coach, Clyde Hart

CONTENTS

ACKNOWLEDGEMENTS

I would like to thank the following people who have helped to make this book possible. First, my wife Armine for all of her support and understanding, and my son Sebastian, who inspires me with his love for reading and his own dream of becoming a writer; my agent Sarah Wooldridge at IMG, whose tireless search for the right publisher and her belief in my ability to write an insightful and informative book has resulted in *Gold Rush*; Jonathan Taylor for understanding my vision for this book and helping to shape that vision; and Linden Gross, my writing coach, who kept me on task and whose energy and excitement about the project were crucial in getting me to the finish line. Thanks to Steve Burdett and Nick Canham at HarperCollins for picking up the ball after the project had started. Thanks also to Nadia Comaneci, Chris Hoy, Rebecca Adlington, Usain Bolt, Sally Gunnell, Sir Steve Redgrave, Mark Spitz, Lord Sebastian

Coe, Ian Thorpe, Cathy Freeman, Dame Tanni Grey-Thompson, Jackie Joyner-Kersee and Daley Thompson for sharing wonderful stories of success, failure, lessons learned and, perhaps most importantly, revealing their personal weaknesses and vulnerabilities.

I would be remiss if I didn't take this time to also thank the people who were instrumental in my own career success. Writing this book brought back many fond memories of challenges, wins, losses and very valuable life lessons learned. My coach Clyde Hart was the only coach I could ever have had. Clyde's approach to coaching as a teacher was a perfect match for my approach to training and competing. I was always trying to learn more about myself as an athlete and Coach taught me everything he knew until the point that we started to learn together. He remains a friend, a coach and a role model. Thanks to my manager and agent, Brad Hunt, who helped me during my career to capitalise on the opportunities that my success on the track afforded me. Thanks to my parents Paul and Ruby, my brother Paul Jr, my sisters Regina, Cheryl and Deidre and our friend Brenda Harris for all of their support and for being the ultimate travelling fan club, following me around the globe and being there for me during all times, good and bad.

And finally, thanks to all of my fans around the world who followed and supported my athletics career over 11 years, and those fans who follow me now as a television pundit and encourage me to continue to share a frank and straightforward perspective on sport.

INTRODUCTION

From the moment the UK contingent unveiled its deceptively simple preview of the 2012 Games during the closing ceremony of the 2008 Games in Beijing, it was clear that this would be Britain's greatest sporting occasion in living memory. London's Games will provide a total contrast to the 2008 Games. Despite the incredible spectacle that Beijing put on during its opening and closing ceremonies, the Games themselves lacked the festive, fun and exciting atmosphere that everyone associates with the Olympics. This time around, we're going to have a celebration of the Olympic spirit and of the athletes, who will have the chance of a lifetime to achieve the apex of their sporting careers.

As somewhat of an honorary Brit, I will be rooting for those athletes from the UK who will have to contend with the monstrous pressure of expectation from a home crowd feverishly anticipating a national gold rush.

Will the more than 500 men and women competing under the Union Jack be able to deliver? British athletes in some sports, like cycling, are poised to capitalise on prior success and the support of Queen and country. But Olympic gold could prove a tall order for many others because the British system of developing athletes, at one time one of the best in the world, has fallen behind over the last couple of decades. And while there have been efforts to get back to where they once were, some of the efforts, in athletics for example, could have been implemented a little too late to have a real effect on the medal haul in London.

On the other hand, this is the Olympic Games, where anything can happen. Even better, this Olympic competition is being held in the UK. A home Olympics is a great and rare opportunity for any athlete. Competing in the Olympics on home soil, if managed properly, can prove competitively advantageous. But capitalising on those advantages isn't easy. This is the toughest sports competition in the world, where the best athletes in the world challenge each other and themselves. As if that weren't enough pressure, this pinnacle of athletic competition only takes place every four years. If successful, your name will be in the history books for ever, and there is no sporting event with a richer history than the Olympic Games. Miss your opportunity, on the other hand, and you may never get another.

Whether you'll succeed or fail, no one knows. But one thing is certain: everyone will be watching. And even as

INTRODUCTION

Olympic stars emerge during the London 2012 Games, other future Olympic champions will catch the dream.

My first experience of seeing an Olympics was the 1984 Games in Los Angeles. It was exciting to watch, but I honestly had no idea that four years later I would be trying out for the US Olympic team, eight years later I would compete in my first Olympics, and 12 years later I would be making Olympic history as the Games returned to the US in Atlanta. My journey through those 12 years included a hell of a lot of fun, a lot of pain, some incredibly rewarding achievements, some major setbacks, and memories that will last the rest of my life. In fact, my entire life is pretty much defined by the events of those 12 years from 1984 to 1996.

This book is not just about my journey but about the journey of many Olympic icons, past and present. You will hear about all of our stories. How we got our start in our respective sports, and our unique journeys to Olympic success. Our failures, our successes and, most importantly, in our own words, our own opinions of how and why we were successful in becoming Olympic champions – in many cases more than once.

Gold Rush attempts to explain what it takes to achieve this very rare level of success, investigating the similarities in the approaches taken by each of the champions, and in the make-up of the champions themselves, as well as the differences between them and their approaches. After looking back at my own road to success and then interviewing more than a dozen Olympic champions to hear their stories and find out more about their road to success, I discovered that the similarities far outweighed the differences. I also confirmed something that I have always felt: that most fans aren't fully aware of the really significant and fine details about their Olympic heroes that make them special. Many Olympic fans have a good 30,000-foot view understanding of Olympic athletes, what makes them tick, and how they achieve such amazing success. This book gets right down to a face-to-face level with Olympic success through the stories told to me – one Olympic champion having a frank, unguarded, casual conversation with another Olympic champion.

I already knew many of these athletes before I interviewed them, and in some cases, as with Seb Coe and Cathy Freeman, they have been long-time friends of mine and we have talked about everything but our Olympic success. So it was truly an enlightening experience for me to talk with these great champions and compare notes not only about our individual Olympic journeys but about what we believe is required for ourselves or anyone else to be successful at the Olympic level. A lot of what I believed already was confirmed from talking with these champions, but I also learned about different approaches from my own that proved successful.

I have always believed that I could put together a pretty good manual for Olympic success. But after talking with so many different Olympic champions who had to overcome multiple different obstacles and challenges en route to their Olympic success, I gained new insight into the mental and physical dedication required to get there.

INTRODUCTION

So as the anticipation of the 2012 Olympic Games rises to fever pitch, let's look at just what it takes to build an Olympic champion.

1.

MY QUEST FOR GOLD

The Olympic Games are the ultimate in most sports. It's certainly the pinnacle of a track and field career. And it was the one prize I hadn't captured. I didn't want my career to be summarised as: *Greatest runner in the 200 and 400 metres ever, but never won an Olympic gold medal.*

I couldn't relax until I had won Olympic gold. But that's a lot easier said than done. I know from experience how you can be totally ready, go into the Olympics undefeated and clearly the best in the field, and still not win. I had gone from being unranked in the world of track and field, which meant that I was not one of the ten best in the world in my events, to being number one in both the 200- and 400-metre sprints. I'd beaten all the best people in the world in both and had gone undefeated that season. That was an accomplishment that had never been done before, and it garnered

1

me the Men's Track & Field Athlete of the Year award for 1990. You can't do better than that.

Two years later, I made the Olympic team. In the four weeks leading up to the Olympics, I prepared for what I knew would be the biggest competition of my life. I focused on the athletes I would be competing against, and worked with my team on how I would need to run the race. Then I prepared to deliver my best.

Not until the opening ceremonies did it really hit me that I was an Olympian. As I looked around at the greatest gathering of athletes representing the best from every nation, I realised even more deeply just how special the Olympics are. This historic competition artfully melds excellence and participation. So even if a country's top bobsledders, for example, don't begin to measure up to the rest of the elite bobsledders in the field, they still get to compete.

As we stood in the Barcelona stadium after marching in as a team, it got really quiet. Then an archer lit his bow with the Olympic flame, which had been carried all around the world by thousands of people during the torch relay, aimed for a cauldron high at the top of the stadium and let go. The flaming arrow soared through the air, landed in the cauldron and lit the Olympic flame, which would burn for the duration of the Games. It was one of the most amazing things I had ever seen.

That would be the last time I would be caught up in the pageantry of the 1992 Olympics. As an athlete, it's not enough just being an Olympian and taking part. You want to succeed and deliver your best performance. For some athletes that might mean winning Olympic gold. For others, it could mean making it to the finals. For some, just delivering the best possible performance on that day is enough. But I was an athlete who was a world champion. I had proven that I could be an Olympic champion. Now I had to deliver.

I was the favourite to win the 200 metres. During the US Olympic trials, which I won, I had missed the world record by a mere .07 seconds. I knew that all I had to do was not screw up the race (which I hardly ever did), execute the right strategy (which I did most of the time), train hard and be prepared (which I always did and I had done this time), and beat a field of competitors who had never beaten me before.

In short, the only way I could lose the gold medal was if I made a mistake or something happened to me. Something did happen.

BLINDSIDED

I had scheduled my last tune-up race in Salamanca, Spain, for exactly two weeks before I would start competing in Barcelona. The night before the race, my agent and manager Brad Hunt and I went to dinner with a Spanish journalist Brad knew from university who was living in Madrid and had come to Salamanca to see Brad and interview me. He suggested a small Spanish restaurant just off the main square. I remember sitting there enjoying a very good traditional Spanish *paella*. We had started the meal with some delicious Spanish ham and olives. As I sat there on that temperate summer night, I remember looking at the ham from which they had carved our appetiser hanging near one of the open front doors which extended from one end of the restaurant to the other, all open. I thought, 'That might not be the most sanitary situation, with cars kicking up dust as they fly up and down the road. This would probably not be allowed in the US.' Just as quickly, I decided that we have too many laws and rules in America, and that I shouldn't worry about it. We even returned there for dinner the following night to celebrate my win. I had wanted to have a really good final tune-up race and I had gotten exactly that. Despite a lack of real competition, I ran 19.91 seconds.

As it turns out, my concern about the restaurant's lacka-daisical attitude to hygiene was justified. By the time we reached Madrid airport the next day I was vomiting. I got on the plane and for the next eight hours I was either vomit-ing, manning the bathroom or sleeping. I felt exhausted even though I had had a full night's rest. Over the next few days I would seem to be getting better only to see the vomit-ing and upset stomach return. Eventually, after about five days of this, my lower stomach and intestinal problems finally cleared up.

FAULTY ASSUMPTIONS
Luckily, my condition hadn't really affected my training, so I wasn't concerned. However, as I was getting dressed on the day I was leaving for Barcelona, I noticed that a pair of pants that had previously fitted me perfectly felt a bit large

4

in the waist. 'That's strange,' I thought. But I didn't really worry about it. I figured I probably had lost a little weight because I hadn't really been eating that much the last few days. No big deal.

When I arrived in Barcelona I got on the scales in the training room. At that point in my career my weight was pretty steady at about 168 pounds, but the scales read 161 pounds. That definitely concerned me. Still, my training was going well, so I felt there was no need to assume that this would affect my performance. So I didn't mention the weight loss to my coach, Clyde Hart, or anyone else. The last thing I wanted at that point was for people around me to start worrying unnecessarily.

The first round of the 200 metres was scheduled for the morning, and the quarter-final would be held later that same day in the evening. I was excited when I woke up the morning of the first round. It was finally race time in my first Olympics and I was the favourite. I had only lost one 200-metre race over the last two years and since my professional career started. I had won the US Olympic trials, a race in which six of the best 200-metre runners in the world had competed. Because each country can only enter three athletes in each event, three of the best 200-metre runners in the world were not competing in Barcelona. I just had to do what I had been doing to get to this point and I would be the Olympic champion.

I went to the Olympic stadium and went through my normal routine to warm up for the first round. After having been in Barcelona for almost a week, I just wanted to get started. When I began to set my starting blocks for the race, I didn't think any more about the fact that I was at the Olympics or that my parents and brother and sisters were all in the stands or what was at stake. As the number one ranked 200-metre runner in the world for the previous two years, and the reigning world champion, I was certainly favoured not just to advance to the quarter-finals but basically to be able to jog through this first-round race and win with ease. Even so, I was all business.

I always approached my first-round races that way, even though I didn't have to since the races are seeded, with the top athletes with the best times coming into the race placed into separate heats. This is done to make sure the top competitors meet in a showdown in the final instead of running against one another in the early rounds. While the competition wasn't stiff, I always chose to use the early rounds to work on different parts of my race. Since my start was the weakest part of my race, I always tried to get out of the blocks with the most explosive start that I could. Then I'd go through the drive phase and the first 50 to 80 metres as if it were a final before relaxing during the remainder of the race in order to conserve energy for the next rounds.

So when the gun went off, I exploded out of my blocks, which were in the middle of the track in lane four. With the exception of Patrick Stephens, a pretty good sprinter from Belgium, I wasn't familiar with anyone else in the race. Although most were the best their country had to offer, they were not truly world-class athletes competing on the international circuit. After I exploded from the blocks with my head still down in the drive phase where I couldn't see any of my competitors, I felt okay but not great.

After driving through the first 20 metres, I came out of the drive phase and started to raise my head – and I was not where I expected to be. In my previous championship first-round races, by the time I raised my head I would have already made up the stagger on the athlete outside of me or even passed him. But I had not made up any of the stagger. I also noticed that I didn't really feel that quick or strong, so I immediately started to put in more effort and press. I got a little response from this effort, but at the mid-point of the race I was not leading, but rather was even with Stevens. Not being able to shake them felt very strange, scary and uncomfortable. I pressed more and was able to get ahead of him and finish first.

I'd won my heat but I felt horrible. I actually felt like I was running in someone else's body. I usually felt extremely fast and very strong, and certainly in control of the race. But on this day I felt that regardless of my effort I hadn't been able to get far enough ahead of the competition.

As I walked off the track to the changing area to take off my spikes and put my warm-up clothes back on, I looked at a television screen that was showing the replay. I wanted to see what I looked like, because I knew I didn't feel good. As I watched the replay I saw that I had struggled the entire way. I didn't look fast or strong, and I certainly wasn't controlling the race.

Now I was really concerned. All at once it hit me and my mind began rewinding through the last two weeks: the scales, my pants not fitting, the vomiting, and all the way back to the initial feeling of sickness in the car driving from Salamanca to Madrid. 'But why have I felt so good in training this past week?' I wondered.

I answered my own question almost as soon as I asked it. In the final week before a major competition you're in what's called a 'taper', where you no longer have the heavy workload and you're now allowing your body to recover and prepare to be at its best for the competition. So the training focus is not on getting stronger or more powerful, the focus is on technique. My training over the last week had been focused on my start and speed. So I never realised that my strength and speed endurance had diminished dramatically during that time.

I met up with Coach after the race. Although we both knew what was happening, Coach always puts a positive spin on things. 'Maybe it's not as bad as it seems,' he said. 'Maybe you just needed to get that one race in to get some rust off. Besides, you're not accustomed to running so early in the morning.' As much as we both wanted to believe his words, we both knew that was in all likelihood not the case.

OUT OF MY CONTROL
I returned to my hotel to rest before the quarter-final, scheduled for later that evening. While I sat in my room that afternoon thinking about what had happened in the first-round race, part of me was really ready to go out and run the next round in order to compete like I normally do. But

part of me was afraid to go back out there and run a substandard race, feeling so helpless and out of control.

When we got back out to the track that evening, I tried to approach my warm-up as if everything was fine and normal. But it wasn't and I was worried. When the race started, I executed the only way I knew how, the same as I always had. I sprang aggressively out of the blocks and drove for the first 20 metres. This was the quarter-final, 32 of the best athletes in the world, so the level of competition was higher than in the preliminary round. When I lifted my head coming out of the drive phase I was behind. I was able to get myself back into the race but only managed to finish second.

I had advanced to the semi-finals, but at this point I was well off the mark and there was no way I could win gold against the best in the world in this type of condition. When I lined up for the semi-final the following day, I knew there was a chance I might not even qualify for the final. Still, the quarter-final had been a better race than the preliminary race, so maybe I could improve in the semi-final and the final.

I set out to do my best, but my best in the semi-final was sixth place. Only the top four advance to the final, so my Olympic dream was over.

After the semi-final I had to go and face the media in a press conference and explain why I wasn't competing at the level I had shown over the last two years, when I had been the most dominant athlete in the entire sport. As tough as it was, I put on a stoic face and explained everything. Inside, however, I seethed with anger. I couldn't believe that this had happened to me. I wondered what it meant for my future. For the last three years I had been one of the top athletes in my sport, demanding the highest appearance fee, rewarded with the most lucrative endorsement portfolio, and commanding respect in the sport as one of its biggest stars. What would it be like not being number one?

When I returned to my hotel after the press conference, Coach, my parents, my brother and my sisters were there waiting for me. They all hugged me and told me they loved me. 'Thanks for coming,' I told them. 'It means a lot to me, but I just want to be alone.' I had no sooner reached my room when there was a knock on my door. I opened it to find my father. If it had been anyone else I probably would have asked them to please let me be alone. But my father has always been my hero and I have always admired him. While he's never been an emotional man or one who shows a lot of his feelings, he always could bring some calm to a situation and say the right thing at the right time to me. So I felt comfortable with him being there with me at that moment.

'Everyone is very proud of you,' he said. 'I know this is tough for you, but I want you to be okay.' I could tell he was really concerned about me. I said, 'I'll be okay.' And as difficult as the days following that semi-final wound up being, I was.

SECOND CHANCE FOR MY FIRST MEDAL

Now, four years later, I had my chance not only to medal in the Olympics but to make Olympic history. Brad and I had convinced the International Association of Athletics Federations (IAAF) to juggle the Olympic schedule so that I could compete in both the 200- and 400-metre sprints. No male athlete had ever attempted to run both.

After six years of intensive training and competitive dominance, I was ready. More than ready. Before the Olympics as usual I'd done my training in Waco, Texas, where my coach Clyde Hart was still the head track coach for Baylor University. I trained there just about every day. During the final week, instead of pushing hard, we focused on the technical elements of the race. We wanted to let my body rest so that it would be fresh for competition. Just days before a competition all of the work has been done, and if it hasn't it's too late to make up the deficiency.

That week I worked on my start out of the blocks, which was never as good as it should have been or as I wanted it to be. The workout, which I had done many times before, was also designed to keep my speed up and to keep me technically sharp. After my warm-up for this particular workout, Coach asked me if I wanted to put on my spikes for the 200-metre portion of the workout. Normally I would definitely wear lightweight spikes for a session requiring me to hit those kinds of times, but this time I decided to wait until we did the starts, even though wearing flats (regular running shoes) would be a disadvantage.

We had a timing system called 'the beeper', which would sound every few seconds during our training sessions to help me ascertain whether I was on the pace the session required, and also whether each interval run was accurate. Just like a metronome that helps musicians develop a rhythm with the music, the beeper helped me accurately measure my speed, so I could pace myself correctly and not go too fast or too slowly. This was critical, since a workout session that calls for three 200-metre sprints to be run in 23 seconds is more effective if each run is actually 23 seconds as opposed to one being 21 seconds, one being 25 and one being 23.

For 15 years I'd heard the beeper, which was wired into the Baylor University track's loudspeakers. I had come to rely on it so much as an essential part of my training that I had my own portable beeper made so that I could take it on the road when I trained away from Waco.

On this particular day I started my first 200-metre run with the beeper set for a 23-second run. I took off. At the 50-metre cone I noticed that I was a little ahead of the beeper. Even so, I maintained my pace. I expected that I would be about the same amount ahead at the second cone, but I was a bit more ahead. I relaxed a little to meet the 23-second goal, but came through the third cone even further ahead. At this point, even though I usually did exactly what Coach's workout called for when it came to times, I decided not to slow down.

I crossed the finish line figuring that I would be about one second ahead and started to count. 'One thousand one.' No beep. 'One thousand –' The beep finally sounded. I was 1.5 seconds fast. 21.5. Not an amazing time, given that I had set the world record a month earlier at 19.66 seconds, but to have done it in a training run, during which I'd tried to relax to get back to 23 pace for the last two thirds of the interval, confirmed that I was in the best competitive shape of my life.

After I finished the run, I saw Coach in the middle of the infield with his stopwatch. He didn't say anything. Normally he would tell me to get back on pace, but this time he remained silent. I walked and kept moving as I always did during the 90 seconds between intervals.

'Thirty seconds,' Coach announced, indicating that one minute had passed and I had just 30 more seconds of rest so I should start moving back towards the starting line. Ninety seconds rest means 90 seconds of rest. Not 100 seconds, not two minutes, but 90 seconds of rest. So you don't start walking to the starting line at 90 seconds. You start running at 90 seconds.

I walked to the starting line and got into start position. The beeper went off and I took off running. I know from experience that the first 50 metres starting from a standing start takes more effort than the other three splits between the other cones, since those segments are from a running start. So normally you start with a little more effort, then settle into a pace and try to relax and maintain it. Since I had run ahead of pace on the first segment of the first interval, I adjusted down and didn't start as aggressively. I passed the first cone at 50 metres. The beeper didn't sound until half a second later. Exactly the same as last time.

'Adjust down,' I thought. However, it's mentally tiring to keep making adjustments during the training session intervals, so I decided to maintain my pace. Besides, I was excited about the challenge of maintaining that pace and that distance ahead of the pace not only for the remainder of that interval but for the third one as well. I finished with about the same time as my previous training intervals – 1.5 seconds ahead by my count.

I looked over at Coach and he said nothing again. I felt really good. I realised I was fitter than I had ever been, because although the final interval was coming up in less than 90 seconds, I knew I could run it in 20 seconds if I wanted to. I wouldn't, since that would be full speed and we never run full speed in training. But the capacity was there.

I started the final 200 and ran just under full effort after having already completed two intervals in the last five minutes. I was well ahead of the first cone when the beeper went off, and it felt effortless. The gap grew at 100 and 150. When I reached the cone at 200 metres, I was 2.5 seconds ahead by my count. That would be 21.5 on the first interval, just under 21.5 on the second and 20.5 on the third.

I started to walk around the track. Coach would normally walk over to join me for the 200 metres back to the starting line side of the track, during which we would talk about how I felt and he would tell me my exact times. This time he didn't. Instead, he walked into the office at the track under the stands. By the time I reached the other side of the track, Coach was walking out of the office, his training log in hand. 'Start your cool down,' he said. Then he showed me the stopwatch. The actual times were 21.4, 21.2 and 20.1. 'And you weren't wearing spikes,' he said.

Coach and I are a lot alike. We expect the best effort, and if that effort is your best, then even if it is as impressive as what I'd just done there's no reason to get all giddy and celebrate. Our attitude was that I had done what I was capable of, so that's what we should have expected. I work with one athlete now who always tells me, when I ask him how training is going, that he and his coach feel they are ahead of schedule. To me that means your schedule is wrong and you need to adjust it! Still, my coach and I both agreed that my accomplishment that day confirmed that I was ready to do something really special in Atlanta the following week. 'The hay is in the barn,' he said. 'We're ready.'

Even so, I sure wasn't going to assume that I would medal. As I'd learned in 1992, I could do everything right and still not win Olympic gold or any other colour. Something out of my control could happen again. Or I could screw it up myself this time.

TIME TO MAKE IT HAPPEN

On the morning of the 400 metres final, having successfully gotten through and winning the first three rounds over the prior three days, I woke up ready to win my first individual Olympic gold medal. I was the overwhelming favourite. Even though I'd be racing against top competitors, including my US team-mate Alvin Harrison, two Jamaicans – Roxbert Martin and Davian Clarke – and Great Britain's

Roger Black, who had also been running well, everyone expected me to win.

I hadn't lost a 400-metre race since I was in college over six years ago. Still, I never took my competition for granted. I didn't believe that any of the athletes in the final could beat me, but I was always aware that there's more to winning a race than being better than the competition. To win races you have to execute, and one little mistake can cost you a race. If something went wrong in this one, would I even be able to race in another four years when the Olympics rolled around again?

On race day I ordered breakfast through room service and began to lay out my uniform, competition number, socks, spikes, music player, headphones, and everything else I would need at the track. Then I sat in my room for the rest of the day visualising almost every scenario that could possibly happen in that final and devising a plan for what I would do in each scenario.

Although we had travelled to the track from the hotel three times prior to the 400 metres final and had gotten the routine down, I wanted to get to the track early, as much to ensure that I was there in plenty of time as to get out of the room. Even though I had always hated waiting all day for a race because I was so ready to run, I usually didn't allow myself to leave my room until it was time to go to the track. But this time heading out early gave me the illusion that I could make race time come quicker.

Finally it was time. I finished my warm-up and prepared to report to the 'call room', a holding room where all athletes in the race are required to report and wait together just before being taken out to the track for the start of the race. Just before walking over, Coach pulled me aside and we prayed together as we had done since I was in college. I had heard other athletes ask God to let them win, which I thought was ridiculous. Coach, however, simply asked God to keep me healthy and, if it was His will, to allow me to run at my best. 'God blessed me with this talent,' I thought as the prayer ended. 'His job is done, and it's up to me and me alone to win this race.'

Coach and I had debated about whether to go for a fast race and possibly a world record in the 400 metres final if I was winning at the halfway point, or to run conservatively since after just a day of rest I had to be ready to run the 200-metre races. The 200 metres would be the more difficult challenge, not only because the competition was tougher but also because it would come after four days of gruelling 400-metre races. 'The decision is yours,' Coach said before I got on the bus that would take us from the practice field to the Olympic stadium five minutes away. I ran through both options in my head and thought, 'Stick to the plan. Don't get distracted with the opportunity to break a world record. There will be plenty of time for that. Win an individual gold medal.'

GOLD RUSH

GOLD MEDAL, GOLD SHOES

I had gotten used to the overwhelming flickers of cameras and the applause each time I walked into the stadium. The attention arose not because I had become the face of the 1996 Olympic Games or because I had announced that I would make history. The attention derived from my decision to wear bright, shiny, gold track spikes, designed for me by Nike. The shoes were unlike anything ever made for a track athlete. The technology and design that went into making these shoes and the time spent, over two years, working on them to make them perfect was incredible. The fans and the media, however, focused on the fact that they were gold and looked like nothing anyone had ever seen before. One magazine actually did an entire story just on those shoes, which could be seen from the top of the Olympic stadium. Opting for gold shoes could have been considered downright cocky, but I was confident and never doubted my ability to deliver gold medals to match my shimmering footwear.

The gold shoes project with Nike had actually started as a result of Nike sprint spikes falling behind those of companies like Mizuno in terms of quality, technology and performance. The last straw had come during the 1993 World Championships when the Nike sprint shoe of 400 metres Olympic gold medallist Quincy Watts came apart in the final 100 metres of the race. He placed fourth in the race and blamed his damaged Nike shoe, which he showed to the world on camera in his post-race interview.

At that point Nike had been making my shoes for three years. Basically they had shoes available to anyone to purchase; Nike athletes would choose from that line of shoes and Nike would make them in whatever colours an athlete wanted, adding their name or any other desired graphic on the shoe. So the customisation of the shoe was purely aesthetic. I had used the same Nike model – a very lightweight shoe with a lot of flexibility that Nike had been making since the 1984 Los Angeles Olympics – from the time I was in university. By 1990, however, Nike had stopped making this shoe and had moved on to much more rigid shoes that were designed to help the athlete's foot strike and recover in a much more efficient way that required less effort. But these shoes were heavy and stiff. I preferred something that would work with my foot and the track.

Although they were no longer selling the shoe I liked, Nike had taken all of the plates (which are the bottom part of the shoe that actually holds the spikes) that they had left in my size and held them in order to make the shoe just for me. Then, at the beginning of 1995, they approached me about a project to highlight the fact that they had over-hauled Nike sprint shoes. In our first meeting about the project, they asked me what I liked about my current shoe and why I liked those attributes. 'What would you want in a shoe if you could have anything you wanted with no limi-tations?' they asked. After I answered, they set out to deliver just that.

Throughout the two-year process the focus was on devel-oping something that would not only be unique to me but would help me perform better by being based on my specific needs, given my body mechanics and the events that I competed in. At one 200-metre race Nike set up high-speed cameras all around the track that were focused on my feet from start to finish. The cameras allowed us to view the actions of my feet during a competition at 1,000 frames per second. This allowed us to really understand the movements of my feet and how the shoe interacted with my foot and the track. We found that the interaction was different on the bend from what it was on the straight. We found that it was different for the left foot versus the right foot. We found that it was different for the 200 metres versus the 400 metres. So we accommodated for all those particulars and developed one pair of shoes for the 200 metres and a different pair for the 400 metres. In both pairs of race shoes, the left shoe differed from the right.

Over that two-year period I would meet with a team of shoe designers about once every month. As we got closer to the 1996 season we met even more frequently. They would come to the track with huge bags of prototypes, using all different kinds of materials, for me to try during training sessions. I would give them feedback and they would make adjustments.

Once we finally settled on a material, the project became really fun. With Nike having invested so much time, money and resources to develop a one-of-a-kind, revolutionary sprint spike, it was a given that the shoe that would make its début on the most popular athlete in the sport as he attempted to make history in the Olympic Games, in front of the biggest consumer market in the world, must look cool, different and special. Nike had been known for years for its marketing mastery and branding genius, and now I got to be part of their decision-making process.

We considered a number of looks, including a clear shoe that made it look like I was wearing no shoes at all. One of the looks we narrowed down to was a reflective, mirror-like finish. Up close it was very shiny and looked really cool. We all liked it. 'It's so bright that it'll stand out and be visible even to people sitting high in the stadium,' one person said enthusiastically.

As I sat in the meeting and thought about that I asked, 'Do you guys think it might look silver?' After silent thought and a minimum of debate, we agreed that a shoe that looked silver would be a problem, given our objective.

'They should be gold,' I thought to myself. Then Tobie Hatfield, a brilliant shoe designer who was the lead on the project and who remains a very good friend of mine today, looked at me and said, 'What do you think about gold?'

I have never been a flashy person. I never wore a lot of jewellery, only a simple gold necklace which I bought with one of my first cheques after I started my professional career. I wore that necklace as something of a good luck charm during every single race in my career and stopped wearing it after I retired. And I also wore a simple gold hoop earring when running the 200 metres and a simple diamond stud when running the 400 metres. So while I don't think anyone would describe me as flashy, they wouldn't characterise my dress or my image as boring or drab. They both pretty much follow my personality. I'm confident but not brash. And while I like to perform efficiently and effectively, that certainly doesn't mean that I'm conservative, either in my running or in my style.

The Nike design team left the meeting, saying that they would return in a month or so with a gold version of the shoe. I never thought once during that time that the shoes would get as much attention as they did or that people would remember them decades later. I never looked at them as a statement; nor did I think even once about the consequence of losing while wearing gold shoes. Failing to capitalise on the amazing opportunity to make Olympic history at home would far overshadow any embarrassment over wearing gold shoes during that attempt. The big question was not whether the shoes' aesthetics would make history, but whether I would. I was about to find out.

RUNNING MY RACE

At ten minutes to the scheduled start time I went through my normal routine, setting my starting blocks and doing one practice start. That was all that was needed. In the 400 metres the start out of the blocks is not as important as in the 200 metres. Because of its greater length there are lots of decisions that have to be made during the race. The critical objective is to limit or if possible eliminate any mistakes. So, after my one practice start, I sat on the box indicating my lane number behind my blocks and ran though the race again in my mind as I waited.

As I sat there waiting for the start, I took the opportunity to look into the stands to get a sense of the atmosphere. The stadium was full, and it made me think for a brief moment about the fact that I was about to win my first Olympic gold medal. That, of course, made me think, 'In order to do that, you can't make any mistakes.' So I turned my attention away from the crowd and back to the race, which was about to start.

The gun went off and I started to execute my race strategy, getting up to race pace as quickly as possible with a good, fast start. The first phase of the race went really well – I made no mistakes and nothing unexpected happened. Feeling comfortable on the back stretch, I tried to relax even more. I focused on Davian Clarke, two lanes outside of me in lane six, because he was normally a fast starter. He didn't seem to be taking much out of the gap between himself and Ibrahim Ismail Muftah of Qatar outside of him. That signalled to me that the athletes outside of me were not running very fast. Then I started to try to get a feel for where Roger Black was behind me. I couldn't look backwards since that would throw me off my own pace, so I started trying to see if I could feel his presence. When I did, I realised that I really wasn't running as fast as I wanted to and I might be a bit off my desired pace.

Normally I would make up the time in the 200 to 300 phase by running harder than normal, but I knew I was in really good shape and I really hadn't felt any fatigue at all at this point. So I adjusted immediately and at about 180 metres started to run at the speed and effort that I would normally move up to at 200 metres. I also decided to really double down on this strategy, and run even faster in this phase than originally planned. I passed the Jamaican Roxbert Martin, then his compatriot Davian Clarke. Ibrahim Ismail Muftah in lane seven dropped out of the race at about 275 metres. As I went around the curve I could only see Iwan Thomas from Great Britain out in lane eight. When I came out of the curve and out of the third phase of the race and went into the final phase with 100 metres to go, I was far ahead of the rest of the field. I knew that I would win this race big.

I continued to sprint down the track just trying to maintain my technique. Normally with 75 or so metres to go, a little bit of fatigue starts to set in. I never felt the least bit tired that day. Since I knew I was going to win the race for sure, I decided to go for the world record of 43.29. I gave it everything I had, crossed the finish line and immediately looked at the clock – 43.49 seconds, my third fastest time ever but still two tenths off the world record. I knew exactly where I had lost it. In the second phase from 75 metres to 150 metres I had relaxed far too much and I knew it.

I thought about that for a second, then realised I had accomplished what I wanted. I had won. I was the Olympic gold medallist for the 400 metres. I no longer had to fear finishing my career as one of the greatest sprinters never to win an individual Olympic gold medal. That brought a smile to my face. I turned around and saw Roger Black, from Great Britain, for whom I'd always had a lot of respect. The look on his face told me he had won the silver medal. We shook hands and congratulated one another.

On my victory lap I started thinking about the 200 metres. I wasn't worried about how I would hold up. 'I could go out right now and run the first round of the 200 metres,' I told the press during my post-race interview. I wasn't exaggerating. I felt that good.

Before the medal ceremony, I was still thinking about the 200 metres as I walked around the holding room. The 400 metres had seemed like a formality, something I had to do before I could get to the 200 metres and make history by becoming the first man to win both in an Olympics. Then Roger came in, his excitement evident. When I mentioned the 200 metres, he said, 'Michael, savour this moment. This is special and you'll want to remember this for the rest of your life.'

He was right. As we walked to the podium, I thought about my parents and brother and sisters in the stands and how much they had knowingly and in some cases unwittingly supported me. I was the youngest, and my three sisters and my brother would always chase me around and tease me. I *had* to get fast!

I turned and saw my family in the stands waving at me. As I stood on the top of the podium, Roger's words crossed my mind again. I looked at the stadium and thought about the fact that I was in Atlanta, in my own country, about to receive my first individual Olympic gold medal. After the officials hung the gold medal around my neck and the US national anthem started to play, I kept thinking about the medal I had just received, where I was and what I had just accomplished. And though I try to be in control and private at all times, I allowed myself to let go and feel the joy, the pride and the relief. That's when I started to cry. I knew that everyone in that stadium and watching me on television could see me, but I didn't care.

I celebrated with my family and friends at a restaurant that night, but couldn't really enjoy the occasion because I knew I wasn't finished. I had the 200 metres coming up and my competitors were certainly not out partying less than two days before the start of an Olympic competition. So I returned to my hotel and climbed into bed.

TRYING TO MAKE HISTORY

After a day of rest, I awoke really early because I had a morning start time for the first round of the 200 metres. I liked morning start times because I didn't have to wait around all day. The quarter-finals would be later that evening. I also liked the idea of getting two races done in one day. Both races went very smoothly. As always, I used them to work on my start and the first 60 metres of the race, during which I tried to make up the stagger on each of the athletes outside of me as quickly as possible as we went around the curve.

The following evening, after winning both rounds the day before, it was time to run the semi-final and final. Normally the semi-final is held in the morning or early afternoon and the final much later in the evening. Instead, we would have less than two hours between the races. Regardless, this would be the day when I would either succeed or fail at what I had set out to do.

The short interval between the races challenged all the competitors in terms of what kind of warm-up to do. On our way out to the warm-up track to get ready for the semi-final, Coach said that he had thought a lot about it and decided it would be best if we went back over to the warm-up track after the semi-final, rest for half an hour, then do a modified warm-up of about 50 per cent of what we would normally do. He felt that in view of this awkward and unfamiliar situation it would be best to stick to our pre-race routine as much as possible. The last thing we wanted during the biggest event of our lives was to create a new pre-race routine even in the face of such unusual circumstances. The decision was a brilliant coaching move.

The semi-final went well. When I came out of the curve far ahead, I decided to slow down and conserve my energy for the final. With 75 metres to go in the semi-final of the Olympics, I was so far ahead I could have stopped running and still win. So that's exactly what I did.

Before the final, I lay on my massage therapist's table for half an hour, running the race over and over and over in my mind. Coach went to see how the lanes had been allocated. Upon his return I tried to ascertain from his face what lane I had drawn. The preference was lane four or five. Coach didn't show any emotion. I think he didn't really care which lane I got because he knew I could win from any lane, but I was intent on running the fastest possible time and wanted every advantage I could get.

Since the 200 is such a short race, I wasn't as concerned about making an error as I had been in the 400. My main concern was trying to run as fast as I possibly could. Lane five, with its gentler curve than three or four, would be perfect. In addition, it would give me the opportunity to have at least one of the faster qualifiers outside of me in lane six as a rabbit. Instead of lane five, however, I drew lane three. Not ideal, but not as bad as it could have been. Besides, Frankie Fredericks from Namibia, a friend and someone for whom I have tremendous respect, Ato Boldon from Trinidad, and the Cuban Ivan Garcia, who was an incredibly quick starter, would all be in the lanes outside of me. That meant three good rabbits!

I put on my headphones, which I always used when I first arrived at the warm-up track to help me get into my own zone and focus, and to minimise distractions. Although I have always enjoyed a wide range of music from jazz to rap, 2Pac was one of my favourite artists. For the 400, I would always listen to some up-tempo R&B; Dangelo was a favourite. But for the 200 I liked to get into a more forceful mode, so I had a playlist of rap music to match the more aggressive approach needed for the 200 metres. For this race, I chose 2 Pac's 'Me Against the World'.

Coach walked over. 'It's time,' he said. I already knew that; I had been looking at my watch every couple of minutes, waiting impatiently for that 30-minute pre-race period to be over so I could start moving again and getting ready. I started to do a modified warm-up which went really well. Then we got back on the bus.

Coach was really serious. I knew he was nervous because he had walked around the warm-up track for almost the entire 30 minutes while I was resting, which was always his tell. He didn't say anything on the bus back to the Olympic stadium; neither did I. With my headphones back on I started to listen to 2Pac again. Same song – 'Me Against the World'. The tempo was slower than I wanted, but it was saying all the right things. I did feel it was me against the world. Everyone else in the race – and in any race I was in – could make their careers from beating me. I couldn't blame them for gunning for me. That's what they were supposed to do.

'Watch your start,' Coach said when we got off the bus, reminding me not to pop straight up out of the blocks, which I tend to do as a result of my naturally more upright running style. Then he just said, 'Go get 'em.'

In the warm-up area under the stadium where the other athletes waited, I checked in again with the officials, then sat in a corner by myself just running the race over and over again in my mind. I started to think about the camera flashes that would accompany my eighth entry into the stadium that week. I had been told that the flashes actually followed me around the stadium as I ran. That then led me to think about how big this would be if I was successful.

I knew what the next thought would be. How big this would be if I failed. Competing in athletics at the Olympic level is probably more difficult from a pressure standpoint than any other sport. With the Games taking place only every four years, the average Olympic athlete might make two Olympic teams in his career. So he has to go into an Olympics knowing that this could be a once-in-a-lifetime opportunity – he may never get another. To compound that sense of pressure, the athlete also knows that it is the biggest crowd he will ever compete in front of, and that the focus at home is on him. Everyone in his country is watching him and wanting him to win. This is not just any other competition.

So then how do you approach it from a mental standpoint? You know that it is special and the history and the magnitude of the Olympics can't be ignored. But if you are to have your best performance, the type of performances you have had to get to this point, you must compete the way you competed in those competitions. So as an athlete you must strike a balance: on the one hand understanding the special nature of this competition and the rarity of the opportunity, on the other preparing and competing the same way you would in any other competition. That's not easy to do, and it takes tremendous mental toughness to strike that balance and to resist the natural temptation to compete harder when the stakes are higher and the opportunity is greater. Competing harder can be dangerous. You can now run tight or overdo the preparation or the execution.

I was certainly at risk in that way. Having just completed four rounds of 400-metre races, including the final just two days before the start of the 200 metres, I was now about to run my eighth race of the Games. Certainly fatigue would have started to set in. I had known all along throughout my preparation and training for this task that it would be difficult and I would have to run a mistake-free race because so much was at stake. But even thinking about the stakes could easily stymie my ability to execute.

I immediately started running the race in my mind again. I knew that when I needed to be focused it wasn't enough to tell myself not to think about things that didn't matter or that were a distraction from the task immediately ahead. That didn't work. I had to, first, recognise immediately when I was becoming distracted, and then replace that thought with something else. And the best something else was always the task at hand. So I always started with the bang of the gun and me reacting to it, and then visualised, step by step, myself executing the race to perfection.

Finally the official notified us that we had five minutes before going out. It was night-time and the temperature was perfect. I put on my spikes and waited. At this point I would always take the opportunity to look at my competition to see if I could gauge their feelings at this moment. Are they feeling confident, afraid or absolutely scared to death? Frankie's demeanour was always mellow, which you might take for scared but that would be a mistake. I knew Frankie well and I knew that the fact that he didn't have an aggressive personality did not mean that he wouldn't run a fast race. Ato Boldon was the opposite. He always purposely carried himself with confidence. But he had never beaten me and I saw nothing in him that made me think today would be any different.

They lined us up according to lane and we walked out into the stadium. I didn't look into the stands despite the flashes going off, but I couldn't help noticing the screams and yells, all of which seemed to be directing me to win this race. 'Go Michael!' 'You're the best, Michael.' 'Give me your shoes!' 'I love you!' Talk about pressure! But I liked being the favourite.

I walked on to the track, sat my bag down and positioned my blocks. 'If I don't run as fast as I know I can, it will be because of my start,' I thought. So I took a practice start, going out about 200 metres. It was a good one. My starts were kind of a mixed bag. Sometimes I would get a good one and sometimes I would get an okay one. Rarely would I get a great one and never would I get a terrible one. I was happy with this one.

I got back to my blocks and settled in for another practice start. I got into the set position and imagined the bang of the gun and took off. I didn't like my second start at all, but I kept running and focused on the drive phase of the race. If a start didn't go well there was nothing I could do about it. I had to move on.

The drive phase went well, but it always did. I never had a problem with that part of the race. I walked back to my blocks, sat down and waited for the command to take our warm-up clothes off. I wouldn't risk another start no matter how dissatisfied I had been with the last one, because that was not part of my routine.

As I sat there I thought about the Olympic 200 metres final I was about to run. Suddenly what had happened during the previous 1992 Olympics in Barcelona flashed in my head. As I normally did whenever I recognised that I had lost focus, I started my automatic default mechanism of visualising myself running the race. But part of my mind continued to dwell on the disappointment I'd suffered in Barcelona. I tried to control my thoughts. 'Your competitors don't care about your disappointment four years earlier,' I told myself. 'They just want to beat you today.'

Finally, I decided to allow myself to think about 1992. 'I have run this race over and over again in my mind a million times and I'm ready,' I told myself. 'I wanted that gold medal in Barcelona so badly. This is another chance to get it. And I'm not going to let anything stand in my way. I'm healthy and ready to go.'

'Warm-ups off,' announced the official. I stopped thinking about 1992 and stripped down to my shorts and tank top. I was happy that I had allowed myself to think about Barcelona. That would be even more motivation for me.

Just moments before the start of the Olympic 200 metres final, I couldn't help but remind myself, 'This is not just any other race. This is a once-in-a-lifetime opportunity. I can win it and I can make history, but to do that I must run a mistake-free race.' Deep into my focus, I thought about the things that I needed to do in the race along with those areas where I was most prone to making a mistake. I knew that Frankie and Ato, both being 100 metres specialists, were better starters than me. I also knew that a poor start induced by my thinking ahead to the 100-metre mark had caused me to lose to Frankie a couple of weeks earlier. Frankie had improved so much lately that I knew I would have to have a greater advantage over him at the halfway point of the race than I had in previous victories if I was going to beat him again.

While that was good knowledge to have before the race, I knew it was a mistake to be thinking ahead. You must take one stage of the race at a time and you must be focused only on the present stage of the race as opposed to two stages or even one stage ahead. Thinking about what I needed to be doing at the halfway mark meant that I wasn't fully focused on the start and reacting to the gun. I vowed I would not repeat the mistake that had cost me a win just 14 days before.

After the introductions, which seemed to take forever, the starter finally called us to the starting blocks. At his cry of 'On your marks' I wanted to get into my blocks right away because I was ready to go. But that wasn't my routine. I hated to be in position and have to wait for someone to finally start getting into theirs, so I always delayed a few seconds.

When I saw that everyone was getting into their blocks, I got into mine and waited. The starter announced, 'Set!' I rose to the set position and focused on the impending sound of the gun. Bang! I exploded out of the blocks.

My reaction time, 0.161 seconds, my best ever, was so good, I wasn't ready for it. I drove my left foot off the rear block, pushed with my right foot on the front block and, with all of the force that I had, thrust my right arm forward and swung my left arm back, keeping my head down all through the first driving step out of the blocks. It went perfectly. Then everything switched and now I was pulling my right foot forward and pushing on the ground with my left foot and driving my left arm forward and swinging my right arm back with equal force as in the first stride. That all went perfectly as well.

Normally this process of driving out of the blocks with these steps goes on for at least ten steps. Ideally, the way the blocks are set up, during these ten steps your body is at a maximum 45-degree angle in relation to the track, which allows each step not to push down on the track but to push against the track, propelling your body forward with each push. In order to overcome gravity, a sprinter must utilise upper body strength and power and exaggerate the swing of the arms to prevent tripping and falling over.

I had shot out of the blocks so rapidly – probably due to a surge of adrenaline along with my intensified focus on the start – that my body bent at an angle deeper than the ideal 45 degrees. And my arm swing was not sufficient to keep up with the angle that I had achieved. That caught up with me on the third step. I was going back to my right foot driving forward, and my left foot had already made contact with the ground and I was starting to push with it. Just as I was switching over I felt my upper body start to fall over. To catch myself and stay upright, I had to shorten my right foot stride to hit the ground quicker than it should have.

I had allowed the moment and what I was about to do to take me out of my normal start which, while maybe not as great as some of the other sprinters, was good for me. I had just gotten the best start of my life, but I couldn't handle a start that good. Focusing on the magnitude of the event and what was at stake, instead of executing the best I knew how, almost cost me Olympic gold and history. Fortunately one of the things that I was always good at and always prepared for is holding composure and getting over mistakes and moving on.

Mistakes are part of competing. You know that they will occur and you always try to minimise them, but when one happens during the race you must move on and determine quickly whether there is an adjustment to be made as a result of that mistake or if you continue with the same plan. I knew that having made a mistake you could not dwell on it or allow it to impact negatively on the rest of your race.

Luckily I had trained myself to deal with mistakes, so despite the stumble I was able to continue executing. I began making ground on the fast-starting Cuban, who I figured had left his best race in the semi-final in which he had come in second. I continued to drive and started to focus on Frankie Fredericks, two lanes outside of me. He was running well, but not making any ground on Ato Boldon, who was also running well.

I stopped thinking about them and focused back on my race, which was going excellently. At 60 metres into the race I was up on the Cuban and gaining on Frankie. I had already taken a lot out of the stagger, which meant that even though Frankie was still ahead of me I was winning the race because he had started ahead of me due to the staggered start. I was beginning to prepare for the transition from running the curve to running on the straight, which would happen at the 90 to 110 metres stage, the halfway point of the race. I was positioning myself so that during that transition I would start to gradually go from the inside to the outside of my lane. In addition to that small adjustment, I also started to gradually straighten up, since my left shoulder was slightly lower than my right as I leaned into the curve. When I came out of the curve I was far ahead of Frankie, Ato and the rest of the field.

At this point I knew I wouldn't see any of the competition again. I also knew that I had won the race. Now it was all about maintaining form. Unlike the end of a 400-metre race, where you try to maintain form and fight against fatigue, in the last 100 metres of the 200 you try to run as fast as possible and maintain your technique, which is everything when it comes to efficiency and quickness. I was going well. Everything had been perfect except for that stumble. I reminded myself to run five metres past the finish line to ensure I didn't slow down in trying to lean.

Five metres from the finish line I felt my hamstring go. Had the strain happened 20 metres earlier I wouldn't have finished the race. But at this point I didn't even slow down, even though it made the injury hurt worse. I only focused on the clock, which stopped at 19.32. Overjoyed, I threw my hands up in the air. 'Yes!' I screamed. I had shattered my old record of a month before. At the Olympic trials I had shaved 12 hundredths of a second off the record of 19.72 that had stood for 17 years. And now I had bettered that by just over a third of a second (34 hundredths to be exact). As the crowd screamed, with everyone on their feet and clapping, I continued to yell 'Yes!'

As I walked back, Frankie came towards me smiling. I shook his hand and hugged him. Then Ato came over and started to bow down to me as he laughed. I hugged him and he congratulated me.

That's when I finally grasped what had really just happened. I had completed the double. Relief, joy and elation swelled. Then I started to feel pain in my hamstring. It had been there since crossing the finish line, but the excitement had overridden the pain. I continued to ignore my leg. At that point I didn't care if it fell off. I had won double Olympic gold!

2.

CATCHING OLYMPIC FEVER

I was an unlikely superstar. I was shy when I was growing up and used to get embarrassed very easily. My biggest fear was always – and to a lesser degree still is – the notion that everyone's laughing at me but I don't know it.

My older brother and three older sisters were the exact opposite, so they teased me a lot and embarrassed me even further by pointing out how I would do anything to avoid embarrassment. They thought that was pitiful. I didn't care what they thought. I just knew that I didn't like the feeling of being humiliated.

Unfortunately as a youngster that happened to me fairly consistently. When I was seven years old I had a friend named James who was the same age and lived two houses down from me. We played a lot, but whenever he didn't like something that I did he would hit me. Each time that happened, I cried and slunk back to my house. When we moved to a new neighbourhood a year later, a kid named Keith, who was exactly like James, took over the role of friendly bully. We played together a lot, but it bothered him that I was better at sports than he was. So whenever he wanted to show me that he was better than me at something, he would want to fight me, because he knew I didn't like to fight. So he would hit me. Once again, I would slink back home instead of retaliating.

My brother and sisters didn't like that at all. Determined that I shouldn't go on embarrassing the family by allowing myself to get beaten up, they tried to teach me how to fight. But I just didn't like fighting. This went on for about three years. One day Keith took my bicycle and wouldn't give it back. When he finally stopped and threw my bike down, I was so angry I punched him in the face. He tried to hit me back but I pushed him down and jumped on top of him and beat the crap out of him. 'Don't stop,' yelled my brother and one of my sisters, who happened to be present at the time. 'How many times has he hit you? Hit him back for every time.' Eventually they pulled me off him and he ran home. After that we played together for years, without a single fight. I had evened the playing field and claimed my own sense of power. I felt good about myself after that and knew I would no longer have to live with that fear and embarrassment of not being able to take care of myself.

Although I could best Keith in sports, I wasn't great in that department. Of course, that's a relative statement. At the informal knockabout games at the park that defined my afternoons and weekends during elementary school, I'd get chosen first by my buddies for soccer and (American) football because of my speed. I was not as good at basketball. Not being considered one of the best didn't sit well with me. So after finishing my homework or in the summers when school was out, I would take the basketball my grandfather had given me and go up to the court to practise shooting baskets. That was the only way I would learn to play better and get chosen first in that sport as well.

Even though I loved playing all sports, I loved experiencing the sensation of speed the most. I loved to run – and run fast. I would ride my bike fast. I had a skateboard and I would ride my skateboard fast. I would find a hill and ride my bike down the hill still pedalling fast, or I would run down the hill because I discovered that I could go faster if I was going downhill.

I was fast from the beginning. I think I first realised that I was fast at age six while playing with a few kids in my neighbourhood. About ten of us had decided to have a race at the park near my house. My friend Roderick who was also six was there, along with some older kids. One of them, Carlos, was my sister Deidre's age, so he had to be about ten or eleven years old. We all lined up and we were running about 50 yards to a football goalpost. One kid called the start. He said, 'On your marks, get set, go!' and by the time he said go half the kids had already taken off. Even though I was late on the take-off, I managed to catch everyone, including the older kids, and won the race. 'I didn't even start on time, and I had to catch you all and I still won,' I screamed to all the other kids. Of course, I had been playing sports with these kids for a while and always got to the ball first. So it was no surprise to anyone that day that I was fast – except me.

Even then, however, there was a difference between outrunning someone on the football field while trying to score a goal, or trying to prevent someone else from scoring a goal, and the lack of any subjectivity or complication in a foot race between me and others. The simple nature of a foot race was appealing to me. There was no skill or technique required at that point. It was simply a question of who was fastest. I wanted to be that person. And most times I was.

I was always very proud of winning. Every year in elementary school we had field day, a competition among all the kids in the school with events like the long jump and 50-yard dash. That was the only event I was really interested in and I won some blue ribbons. I remember one particular field day my mother had come up to the school to watch me participate. I won the race and looked over for her reaction. She was clapping and smiling as she nodded her head to me in approval. Having my mother there to watch me felt really good. I couldn't wait to get home to hear her tell me how proud she was.

After school was over I ran home with my ribbon. I showed it to her as soon as I burst through the door. She looked at it, told me I had done a good job, then told me to get started on my homework and do my chores. That was the balance my parents showed. They were happy for me to participate in sports if it made me happy, but they never got carried away with it.

In addition to the school field days I also participated in a parks and recreation summer track programme called the Arco Jesse Owens Games. Every neighbourhood had a park, and in the summer kids from all the parks would come together and be grouped by age so they could compete against one another in different track and field events. I competed in the 50-yard dash and 100-yard dash. The first summer my sister Deidre and I participated in the Arco Jesse Owens Games, I had been the fastest in my age group at my park but finished in the middle of the pack at the Games. I didn't like that feeling. I didn't even know the other kids. I didn't know if they were better than me. I just knew that I wanted to win and I had a strong belief that I could win. I told myself I would try harder the next time I had an opportunity to race. I honestly didn't know what else I could do in the face of defeat.

Winning races had come easily to me up to that point. Looking back on that day, I think I was just so accustomed to winning the races I had run in my neighbourhood and at school that I expected to win. I knew I was fast and I liked the feeling of winning. I liked being good at something and I liked the attention I got from being fast.

Of course, I didn't share that with anyone.

FAMOUS PERSONALITIES

'If you look at most sportspeople – and this is the trend, not the absolute – they tend to be more introverts,' says Sir Steven Redgrave, five-time gold medallist in rowing. 'They tend to be more interested in what they're doing – very quiet from that point of view.'

He speaks from personal experience. Like me, Steve was shy when he was growing up. 'As a kid and even as a teenager, I wouldn't say boo to a goose,' he says. Heavily dyslexic, Steve, who had two older sisters, struggled with schoolwork. Sports – any kind of sports – became his outlet. 'Even if I wasn't that good at it, I still enjoyed doing it, because it was like freedom in some ways.' So he played, in his words, 'a little bit of football' (or soccer for you American readers) for a team that was good enough to have a couple of its players go on to apprenticeships at professional clubs. 'Little' was the operative word since as reserve goalkeeper he sat on the side most of the time. He also 'messed around' with rugby week in and week out, playing on a team that needed volunteers from the football team to make up the 15 players required for a match. And as a competitive sprinter during junior school, he was one of the fastest in his home county of Buckinghamshire.

His sports escape routes broadened when the head of the school's English department introduced Steve to rowing. 'Our school was mainly a soccer school. Because he had a love for rowing, he used to go around and ask a few individuals if they'd like to give it a go. I hated school, so being asked to go out on the river in a games lesson once a week was a no-brainer from my point of view. The only problem is after two or three weeks we started going down every day after school. He asked 12 of us from my year. Within two weeks there were only four of us left that were committed to doing it.

'He just made it so much fun. It wasn't about maybe going to the Olympics or even racing anywhere; it didn't even cross my mind. It was just about doing something a bit different that the other kids in my school didn't get the opportunity to do.'

That first time out, Steve won seven out of seven races. Even though that gave him confidence, 'I still wouldn't have gone in town and told anybody,' he says.

Daley Thompson may well be Steve's polar opposite. A supremely confident athlete from the start, Daley made his mark in the 1980 Moscow Olympics by winning the decathlon, which consists of ten track and field events: 100 metres sprint, long jump, shot put, high jump, 400 metres sprint on the first day, and 110 metres hurdles, discus throw, pole vault, javelin throw and 1,500 metre race on day two. He then followed it up by successfully defending his title four years later in the 1984 Games. These Olympics were considered to be the Carl Lewis Games, because Lewis had established himself as the greatest track and field athlete since Jesse Owens. In fact, Carl was attempting to duplicate Jesse Owens's amazing history-making moment from the 1936 Olympic Games in Berlin, when he won gold in the 100 metres, 200 metres, long jump and 4 x 100m relay. And Carl was attempting it in his home country during the Los

Angeles Games. Daley, however, thought he was the better athlete and that the world should know. So he created a T-shirt, which he wore to the press conference after winning his second gold medal, which read: 'Is the world's second-greatest athlete gay?'

Although he later insisted that 'gay' meant 'happy' and that he hadn't necessarily targeted Carl Lewis with the statement, the brash move created a firestorm. Fortunately, during his career his athletic performance was so superior that the sporting headlines outshone the others.

Daley was a very good athlete from the very beginning. He played football and found that he was superior athletically to the other kids. He would discover the same thing when he wandered down to the local track club a couple of times a week at the age of 15. He was so good that he actually made the British Olympic track team the following year and found himself competing at the 1976 Montreal Olympic Games on his birthday. 'Day one of the decathlon was my birthday,' he recalled. 'I was 16 on the first day and 17 on the second day. I didn't win that year, but just being on an Olympic team and having that Olympic experience was the most fun I ever had.'

Paralympian Tanni Grey-Thompson, who won a mind-boggling 16 Olympic medals including 11 golds, garnered a bronze medal during her first Olympic Games. She would go on to compete in four more Games, a feat as astonishing as her medal count.

'I remember watching the 1984 Games on TV and thinking, "Wow, that would be really good to do that,"' she told me. She had realised that she wanted to seriously compete in wheelchair racing several years earlier after participating in a race and coming in fourth. That proved to be a defining moment for her. 'At that moment, everything else took second place,' she recalls. Racing was exhilarating and fun. Not winning, however, was not. She says, 'I remember thinking, I want to be better; I don't want to come in fourth again.'

Over the next three years she continued to race competitively without making much of a mark. 'In 1984 I wouldn't have been on the radar of anybody,' she says. 'But as I watched the Games I thought, "I could do this if I worked really hard."

'I remember getting the letter saying I had made the 1988 Olympic team. I was at university and I'd come home for the Easter holidays. I came in through the front door on Saturday morning and my mum said to me, "There's a letter there from the Paralympics Association." I picked it up and looked at it, turned it over, and opened it. It said, "Dear Tanny, Congratulations." I just screamed. My mum was like, "What? What?" I was hoping I'd make the team but I wasn't expecting it. I'd made big improvements through 1987 and 1988 in terms of where I was in the world. But at 19 I was right on the borderline for going. So they took a real chance with me.'

Most people catch Olympic fever and work as hard as they can to earn a spot on the team. Daley's success happened so fast that making the team provided him with the inspiration that would fuel him in the years that followed.

'What was your first memory of the Olympics?' I asked.

'Watching Valeri Borzov on TV in the 1972 Olympics,' he said. 'I was really impressed with Borzov and how he carried himself.' As Daley recalled, Valeri, a Russian 100-metre runner who was known as being a really tough competitor, 'delivered a really great piece of work'.

As a two-time gold medal decathlete competing in ten different track and field events, Daley would go on to become the greatest athlete of his time. When I asked him about how he dealt with the pressure, he said, 'I never felt pressure.'

I wouldn't believe that from a lot of athletes, but I believe it with Daley. I don't think he felt pressure, because where does the pressure come from? It comes from being afraid that you're going to underperform – not necessarily compared to what other people expect but in terms of your own expectations. But Daley didn't care. He just figured, 'If I lose, I'm going to come back and I'm going to win the next time.'

Sprinter Usain Bolt says much the same thing. 'People always say, "Why are you not worried?" I said you can't be worried. If you're the fastest man in the world, what's there to worry about? Because you know you can beat them. All you've got to do is go execute,' he told me when we talked in Jamaica in 2009. 'I'm not saying every day you're going to get it perfect, but if you're fast there's no need to worry. If you've had a bad day, you just had a bad day. Next time you bounce back.'

Despite his antics on the field, Usain isn't exactly an extrovert. He prefers to chill at home or in his hotel room rather than to go out on the town. But when it comes to introverted champions, Cathy Freeman has us all beat.

Cathy's *quiet* and *reserve* (her words) define the word *calm* (my word). And yet she's won gold in two World Championships, four Commonwealth Games and the Olympic Games on her own home turf.

She discovered the Olympics at age ten, while watching a made-for-television movie about American indigenous distance runner Billy Mills, who won a gold medal in the 10,000 metres during the 1964 Tokyo Games. 'I was at an age where, oh, there's a runner who's indigenous and American, and he's sort of similar to the indigenous people over here,' Cathy told me. 'I set in my mind that I wanted to be a runner when I grew up.' Watching the 1984 Los Angeles Olympic Games unfold the following year cemented that aspiration. By then, thanks to her stepfather, she already had the words 'I am the world's greatest athlete' posted on her bedroom wall.

That set the bar. 'In 1990 I made my first Australian team for the Commonwealth Games,' Cathy told me. 'Two years later I went to Barcelona. Each year that went by, it became clearer to me where I had to be and what I had to do, the sort of person I had to become.'

GOLD RUSH

TUNING IN TO THE OLYMPICS

A number of Olympic champions fell into their sports and went on to make history. For many, watching the Olympics served as a catalyst. Mark Spitz, who holds a remarkable nine Olympic gold medals in swimming, didn't join a swimming team because he loved the sport or had been inspired by the Olympics. At least not at first. At the age of nine his mother had put him into a YMCA camp programme just to give him something to do. The problem was that the programme involved arts and crafts instead of sports. Mark, and the friend who had also been put into the camp by his mother, 'didn't want to sit around with a bunch of girls doing stupid stuff'. It turned out that a brand new swimming pool had just been completed and programmes would begin being offered the following week.

Mark told me about what happened next. 'On the very first day in the class that I was in, the instructor said for everybody to line up. They put us all alphabetical and they told us to jump into the pool and hold on to the side. So we were all on the length of the pool and the instructor said, "When I call your name, I want to see how you swim across the width of the pool." Well, it was a heated pool, but when you fill up a pool, the first day or so, it's not really heated, so I was freezing my butt off. By the time they got to the S's all I did was swim across the pool without stopping. Little did I know that the guy who was the instructor of that class was looking to see who didn't stop. He had set up criteria, unannounced to anybody, that if you didn't stop he was going to ask you to go out for the swim team. Well, my

50

buddy, his last name was Cooper, got halfway through the width of the pool, stopped and looked at me and was waving and showboating – 'Ha ha, I got to go first!' – because that's what your buddies do, right? So he never got asked to go out for the swim team. There were probably four people in that one session that didn't stop for whatever reason.

'So I went out for the swim team. I didn't know a whole hell of a lot about swimming at the YMCA level. It was designed as a novice programme. At the end of that summer programme we went to a swimming meet. I don't even remember what I was swimming, but I remember that it was time-based only. My mom took me over to the end of the pool where there were three circles on the deck that said 6-5-4. There was also a little staircase that said 3-2-1. They put me on circle number 5 and handed me a purple ribbon. I looked to my left and I noticed the guy that was on the staircase, he got a white ribbon. The guy on the next step up got a red ribbon, and the guy at the top got a blue ribbon.

'I came back to my mom crying and gave her that purple ribbon. That was the first time I recognised that I would get a reward for doing something in a sport. I didn't understand about why I got the reward, or even that someone had given me a time or had a stopwatch on me. The fact was that I didn't like the purple ribbon because it was quite obvious that that guy on the staircase with the blue ribbon had been treated as more special than I had. I wanted to be on that top stair. How was I going to get there? I had no clue. But I know that to this day I don't like purple.'

Ironically, Ian Thorpe, who hopes to add to his five gold medals in the 2012 Olympics, also fell into swimming. 'My sister swam. She only swam because she broke her wrist, so the doctor recommended she swim to strengthen her wrist, but she ended up being quite a swimmer. She made our national team. When I was young, I basically decided I'd take up swimming because I was really bored being dragged along to all these swimming carnivals by my parents to watch my sister.'

Ian already played a few different sports at the age of eight, and it's probably safe to say that he was better at most of those than he was at swimming. 'When I was young I wasn't that good a swimmer,' he told me. 'I was allergic to chlorine, as well, and was getting sick from being in the pool. But I enjoyed it. My mum had to take me to the doctor, and basically the doctor said, "Your son's allergic to chlorine. It has to do with how the adenoids mature in your nose. When he hits puberty it's not going to be a problem as much any more. If you think he's going to be a champion swimmer, it's probably advisable that you have them taken out."

'My mother didn't think I'd be a champion swimmer, so we opted to do nothing and I continued to get sick from swimming from time to time. That took me out of the pool every once in a while. In the pool I had to wear a nose clip, which is probably the uncoolest thing you can wear when you train. But I was like the nerdy swimmer when I was little.

'My parents wanted me to stop swimming, figuring it wasn't good for me. But by the time I was ten or eleven I was pretty much winning everything in the pool in the age group competitions. By the time I was 14 I made the national team. I missed every development team on the way because I didn't meet the criteria. I was usually too young. At 14 I went away on my first trip, which was the Pan Pacific Championships in Japan, and came second. Then, the following year, I was world champion. The year after that I set four world records in four days. Then, the following year, I was Olympic champion.

'As a pre-teen, my goal was to become an Olympic athlete. I dreamed of winning Olympic gold. At that point, however, I thought maybe Athens would be the first place that I could go and then look at the Olympics after that. My winning the World Championships at 15 was a shock to everyone around the world, and it was a shock to me as well. I'd done things in training that no one else had done, and I was the deserved winner at that race. At the time, however, I just thought I was doing these laps. I didn't know how it would equate to a performance that meant that I was world champion. I didn't realise that that win probably meant that I would be favoured to win at the 2000 Olympics. I didn't even realise I'd make the team.'

TAPPING ONE'S GIFTS

Mark and Ian may have fallen into their sports, but they sure made the most of the opportunity. I believe that everyone, no matter who, is blessed with a natural talent and ability to do something well. It may be running fast like me, it may be overall athletic ability in all sports, it may be mathematics, it may be teaching, it may be an incredible ability to remember and recall things. Maybe it's something that one can use to make a living with. Maybe it's something that you love to do, especially since as Steve Redgrave points out, 'the better that you find you do something, the more you enjoy it, and the more you like doing it, the more you get success from it. It's self-propelling in some ways.' In the case of most Olympians, including me, it is a combination of both.

Some people never find their inborn gifts, some find them late in life, and some, like me, are fortunate to find them early on. I was very lucky that when I was growing up we spent most of our free time in my neighbourhood playing games and sports with the other kids. That's how I discovered that I was fast. Even then, however, had I just followed what my friends did, I would have only played football, which is like a religion in Texas. I would never have found my love for track as a sport and never would have discovered just how good I could be, which ultimately turned out to be the best in the world.

That is why I encourage my own son, and any young people I talk to, to try different things. But that's not the national trend. Instead of competing in after-school pick-up games, most kids these days grow up playing organised sports as part of youth teams and leagues which have become big business. As a result, most of the kids who come into my sports performance training centre, Michael Johnson Performance, have already started to specialise in one sport as early as age ten, so they lack the athleticism that we kids from the seventies developed from playing multiple sports. I developed my speed from sprinting, for example. But I also developed explosive power, which helped me to be a better sprinter, from playing basketball. I developed my quickness – the ability to make short bursts of speed in different directions – from playing football.

The kids who specialise early also never get to search out what really stirs them. I want my son to play a sport, to learn to play an instrument, and to try new things, so that he can discover what he is passionate about and in what areas he is gifted. Of course everyone believes that because he is my son he must be fast, and they immediately ask about his speed and whether he's going to be a sprinter. But the fact that he's my son doesn't automatically make him naturally gifted at athletics or any sport. And it certainly doesn't guarantee that he will be passionate about – or even like – athletics or sports. I understand that, so the last thing I would do is push him to participate in athletics or try to become an Olympic athlete. It is his life, and it's up to him to decide what he wants to do with it and to discover what he enjoys and what talent he is blessed with.

At this point in his life (he's 11) I do mandate that he participate in some sport, since I know that there are incredible lessons to be learned from taking part in sports. But I give him the right to choose which sport. If he decides to get serious, I'll make sure he has the coaching support that he needs. But we won't be talking about the Olympics or any other top-level competition right off the bat.

Unfortunately, too many parents and/or coaches these days do exactly that, telling students that they can aspire to the Olympics or the NBA or the Premier League the moment they show any promise. As a result kids are aiming for the Olympics or professional sports before they've even won their school's championship.

NOT SO FAST

Even those high school athletes who are highly sought after by the Colleges start getting ahead of themselves. Right away they start thinking Olympics, they start thinking professional career, they start thinking endorsement contracts and deals. There's a danger to that, which we'll explore at length in Chapter 4. Conversely, focusing on how to improve performance instead of where that performance might lead seems to contribute to the kind of success that builds Olympic champions.

As a teenage competitor, I just wanted to be the fastest 16-year-old in Dallas. To my benefit, I didn't think beyond that. I'm far from being the only Olympic late bloomer. For many Olympic champions the notion of even participating in – let alone winning – the Olympics took a while to set in.

'I think I ought to say something to you,' Sebastian Coe's father and coach Peter said to his son on a rain-soaked night in the late 1970s as they walked off the training field. The middle-distance runner readied himself to hear a message about the training session he had just completed or his upcoming race. Instead, his father said, 'I think you're going to go to the Olympic Games. I've watched people get to Olympic Games and not deal with it that well, and I'll just guess maybe it's something we ought to start thinking about.' Seb just smiled. Although the notion seemed too improbable to take seriously at the time, he would go on to set eight outdoor and three indoor world records in middle-distance track events and win four Olympic medals, including the 1500 metres gold medal at the Olympic Games in 1980 and 1984.

Even though I didn't see myself as an Olympian at first, I always thought I would do something special. Although my family didn't have a lot when I was growing up, I figured I would be successful. I assumed, however, that my dream of controlling my own situation, having the things I wanted and travelling would come from having my own business. I had no dream of being a professional athlete. And since I spent most of my time playing outside rather than watching a lot of television, I really knew nothing about the Olympics.

Until well into high school, sport was just something I did for fun. Sure I liked being the fastest. But there was no strategy involved. I just went out to competitions and started running when the gun went off. Then in my final year of high school, as the best on my high school team, people started to talk about my potential to be district champion, regional champion, or maybe even state champion. The biggest prize for a high school athlete is being a state champion. In order to compete to be a state champion you have to finish in the top two in your district. Then you advance to your region and must finish in the top two in the regional competition. I lived and competed in the hardest district in the country, so just advancing out of district was extremely difficult. There would be kids that I was a lot faster than who would get to state because they came from an area where there weren't many fast athletes. I had to learn how to compete when you are up against athletes who are similarly or equally talented.

This was the first time I started to have to think about how I was going to beat other athletes. How was I going to run faster than them? I had to learn to prepare to compete against them. If a racer was in front of me and I had to go get him, what should I do? Did I just try harder? Did I need to be patient?

You need to think about those things before the race starts. In addition, because you know the athletes you're up against, you know what they're capable of, it makes you nervous. How do you deal with that? And how do you deal with the expectations and the pressure and still deliver your best performance? When you put all of that together, what you're doing is learning to compete.

I would have to wait a few years for that. By the time I was 13 I was already faster than everyone on my school track team, but in competitions against other schools I would win some races and lose some races. I won more than I lost, but when I lost I was disappointed because I didn't like the feeling of losing any more as a young teenager than I had as a youth. I don't know what it was that I didn't like about losing other than the fact that if I was losing, then I wasn't winning, and I liked winning.

At that point in my life I didn't know what to do about losing except to work harder at whatever drill my coach was giving me during practice each day, and to try harder in the races. This seemed to help somewhat but still didn't guarantee me victory every time.

What I know now, as an owner of a performance training company training youth athletes between the ages of 9 and 18, is that it's between 12 and 15 that most kids will make a major leap in their natural athletic ability. Some will develop faster than others. I remember that one of the kids I beat the first time I raced him proceeded to beat me every other time we raced. I don't know what his real name was, but he went by the name Tank. As his name might indicate, he was bigger than me. I remember that he had very thick legs and already had a moustache. Knowing what I know now, I would say that Tank was probably a bit ahead of me in his development.

I took two years away from sport from the age of 14 when I first started high school. My school was a special career development school that only accepted the best of the kids who applied, and each student chose a career focus from many different offerings. At the time I dreamed of becoming an architect, so I spent half of the day learning about that particular career. Eventually I missed sport and came back to track.

When I started competing again at the age of 16, having not played any sports for two years, I had made a big leap in my athletics development, in large measure because I had matured physically. I was immediately winning races easily and working hard which had become standard procedure for me. But I still wasn't winning every race and I still hated that. In my third year of high school I had won every race until the district championship which I lost, finishing third, and it ended my season. Roy Martin and Gary Henry, who were older than me by one year and in their final years of high school and also very good athletes, had both finished ahead of me.

GOOD COACHING HELPS

The more I thought about why I had lost, the more I put together different things I had heard from other people about the impact that good track coaches who trained their athletes all year could make. My coach, Joel Ezar, was a wonderful man with whom I had a great relationship. But he was not a great track coach; he was a football coach who coached track in the spring when the football season was over. So I simply wasn't as ready as those other athletes I was losing to. In addition, they knew more about what they were doing on the track than I did.

I didn't know what to do about the coaching gap, but believed that I could solve it by working harder. The next year, my final year of high school, two other athletes/ friends and I began to go out on our own after school and run. We didn't really know what we were doing but we didn't know that. We just felt that if we worked in the autumn instead of doing nothing we would be better in the spring.

I hadn't yet developed my absolute hatred for losing (rather than mere dislike of it). Even so, I was always looking for a way to prevent myself from losing. Throughout my life, as I matured and moved from one level of training and competing to the next, it became clearer exactly what I needed to do to be the best I could be. I just always believed that if I was the best I could be, I wouldn't lose.

I've always said, and I always tell athletes, that if you run your best race and you lose, you have nothing to be ashamed of or disappointed in. I still believe that. But I, personally, never had a loss where I felt it was my best race. Even when I competed to my best ability in high school and lost, I didn't feel it was my best race because I didn't feel I was as prepared from a training standpoint as I could have been. A big part of my decision when I was deciding which university to compete for was which coach would be able to help me achieve my best.

In spite of not having a real track coach during my high school career, I still managed to win both the district and regional championships. At the state championship I finished second in the 200 metres behind Derrick Florence, who still holds the high school record for 100 metres and to whom I would never lose again. I wasn't happy about not winning, but I was more excited that I would be competing at college than I was disappointed that I had lost the state championship.

Originally I viewed the track scholarship I'd accepted from Baylor University only as a means to go to a better college than I would if I had to pay for it myself. But in

1986, between high school and college, I finally start thinking about professional track. I was working in an office that summer, when I started seeing newspaper headlines about the US Olympic Sports Festival in Houston. Reading about Carl Lewis, Calvin Smith and Floyd Heard arriving in Houston to compete in this high-level competition triggered my initial aspirations to run and compete professionally. After finishing the article I found myself for the first time daydreaming about competing against the best in the world and envisioning myself being at this competition with these athletes. I started to really believe that I could be great, because I knew that I hadn't reached my full potential in high school.

At Baylor University I was in a serious training programme for the first time. It was tough in the beginning. I hated the weight workouts, which I avoided. But I loved training on the track each day and looked forward to it. I approached each day like a competition because I could feel myself getting stronger and better.

AIMING HIGH, HIGHER, HIGHEST

Even though I made some great strides during my first year, I got injured at the end of the season and wasn't able to compete in the NCAA (National Collegiate Athletic Association) university championships. So the following year I focused on becoming an NCAA champion. I hadn't even considered higher-level competition – let alone the Olympics – until one of my team-mates, Raymond Pierre, went on to compete in the US national championships after the college national championships. Raymond did really well at the US championships, finishing fourth in the 400 metres. This earned him a position on the US national team for the 1987 World Championships, which would be held later in the summer in Rome. Raymond spent most of the summer in Europe competing on the international circuit and once competed as an alternate for the US team, running in the preliminary round of the 4 x 400 metres relay team that won the gold medal.

The day he returned from Rome, school had already started and the team had already started training. Raymond came out to the track wearing a USA team uniform shirt. The only way to get your hands on any official USA track team gear was to make a US team, which was a great accomplishment, so having the gear was a badge of honour. I had seen in my freshman year a handful of athletes from other universities who had competed on US teams wearing USA team gear, and I wanted that. It seemed really cool, because it showed the accomplishment, and signified how good the athlete was.

Raymond was an athlete whom I knew well and who had become a friend. He was the only person I knew personally who had actually competed on a US national team and on the professional international circuit. After practice he invited me over to his apartment. When I got there he was still unpacking his bags. He had become a Nike-supported athlete, which meant that since he wasn't a professional athlete yet they couldn't pay him but they could send him all the shoes and gear he wanted. He had bags of new Nike gear and USA team gear. He had picked up gifts that were given to him at the international competitions he had taken part in. There were CD players too, which in 1987 was a new technology and a very cool thing to have.

My eyes opened as wide as the Olympic medals I would eventually earn. I couldn't believe all of the free gear and gifts he had received. And he had actually had the experience of competing on a US team and the international circuit, which he told me all about. I wanted that experience myself. To top all of that off, a week later Raymond drove up to practise in a really cool new red scooter. Those had become really popular in the US then, and he had been able to buy it with the expense money he received from his trip to Europe. I was hooked and needless to say inspired. I asked Raymond questions for weeks after his return, and he was happy to share every detail of his trip and experience with me.

Unlike me, some Olympian champions caught Olympic fever early on. 'That's what I want to do in life,' Sally Gunnell realised at the age of 14 as she sat glued to the television during the Moscow Olympics watching anything that moved. Entranced with Nadia Comaneci and Olga Korbut, she decided to join a gymnastic club. Only after another girl at her school announced that she was going down to athletics did Sally decide to go along. 'I thought it would be better to go with somebody rather than go on my own,' she recalls. So she joined the athletics club and went on to win a gold medal in the 400 metres hurdles at the 1992 Olympics.

Steve Redgrave found success so early in his rowing career that he simply assumed winning the Olympics was inevitable. 'The first year, we thought we were brilliant,' he says. After just messing around in the water, the team had entered their first race for fun and actually won. The following season they entered seven events and won all seven. 'We were God's gift to rowing,' he said. By the time Steve was15 people had begun to tell him, 'You're really good at this. One day you could be a world champion.'

'I thought, "World champion sounds nice; why not Olympic champion?" I knew I wanted to be an Olympian, because I was the best in the country. Why not?'

That sense of inevitability would prove to be both his great motivation and, initially, his downfall. 'I figured, "All I've got to do is follow what the coaches are telling me to do and it will happen,"' he recalls. 'It wasn't until 1983 when I went to the senior world championships as a single sculler and I got eliminated – I didn't make the top 12 – that I suddenly thought, "I am good domestically, I'm okay internationally, but not the same sort of level as people are saying I am good at." Suddenly it dawned on me that if you have an ability you've got to bring that ability out. It's about how hard and how well you prepare. That was the turning point in my career.' It would also prove to be the turning point in his life, transforming him from 'shy goose' to confident five-time gold medallist.

GOLD RUSH

RUNNING INTO THE RECORD BOOKS

Jackie Joyner-Kersee, the Greatest Female Athlete of the 20th Century according to *Sports Illustrated for Women* magazine, was the opposite of shy from the very beginning. 'I was very outgoing,' she told me. 'I was one who would put my phone number down and have people contact me, and my mom would have to tell me, "You stop putting your number down on everything, because I'm tired of all these strangers calling the house." Because I wanted to be involved in everything.'

Jackie, three-time Olympic gold medal winner who would become one of the all-time greats in women's heptathlon and long jump, thought she was good at track and field from the moment she and her sister signed up at the community centre. She had long legs and could jump high. Of course she was good, the nine-year-old reasoned. 'My first race, I finished last,' she told me. 'That challenged me to really continue to run. Then some of my friends made the relay team. I wanted to be on the relay team but I was number six or seven. So I just set my sights on trying to improve a tenth of a second if I was running or half an inch if I was jumping. That was to let me know I was getting better, that the work I was doing was paying off.

'I didn't really know what a track looked like, because we ran in a park, and we ran on cinder. This park had just one big dirt track around. The coaches told us it was about 400 metres, but as we got older we realised it was like 1,200. When you're younger they can pull that stuff on you. I could never finish the lap, and I was like, wow! So the goal was to try to go one lap around without stopping. All this started at the age of nine. It wasn't until I was 14 when I saw the 1976 Olympic Games on television that I saw girls doing what I was trying to do. That's the first time I ever saw girls or women on TV doing sports. I thought, "Maybe I will go to the Olympics one day."

'It was really the idea of being on television that most attracted me. For real! I *had* to get on TV and it seemed like everyone was talking about the Olympics. Our coaches told us to watch. I saw sprinter Evelyn Ashford [win gold]. I saw Nadia Comaneci who was the same age as me earn a perfect score. At that time I was like, "I'm going to be a gymnast, too."'

The gymnast fantasy came and went, but Jackie's dedication to track and field held firm. Although Jackie didn't know if she could ever be good enough to get to the Olympics, even imagining the possibility motivated her. Besides, hanging out at the community centre and doing sports got her away from home, which she found hugely appealing. Mostly, however, she just wanted to see whether hard work would continue to yield progress. 'I practised hard, and the results were coming. It took me a while to get out of last place and then sixth place, but the placement didn't matter to me because I saw my times improving.'

It didn't take long for people to start recognising Jackie's potential. 'People would say, "You're gifted. You're talented." But I really didn't know what all that meant. I was kind of rough in those days. I would fight another girl because she was seeing my friend's boyfriend – all kinds of crazy stuff that would get me into trouble. One day the Assistant Principal pulled me off a girl I was fighting and said, "Get up to my office." When he got there he told me, "You know, we expect better things out of you." I'll never forget that. It was like, wow, people see some greatness in me.'

That helped Jackie decide to commit to her training in a serious way. 'I remember telling my girlfriends when I was in junior high school that I was going to go to the Olympics. They thought I was crazy. From that day on I said to my friends, "No, I can't meet with y'all." We were basically a gang, and I just knew that wasn't good.'

As luck would have it, her school started complying with Title IX, legislation guaranteeing girls the same access to sports as boys, which had been enacted four years earlier, just in the nick of time for Jackie. 'My first year in high school, which would have been my sophomore year, we couldn't practise until 6:30 p.m. after the boys finished their practice. My mom, who was really strict, wasn't going for that. I'm going to come home and then go back up to the school and practise? She wasn't feeling that at all. My mom was just going to pull me out of sports altogether because her philosophy was that I had to be home before the street-lights came on. Then the coaches started pushing the Title IX issue because they said that wasn't right. From there, they changed it so that we could practise before the boys. That made a big difference.

'My mom didn't really understand what I was doing athletically. My dad understood. If it wasn't for my dad telling my mom that it was okay, I probably wouldn't have been doing sports at all. She didn't care about me doing any sports and didn't know the first thing about running around a track. My mom worked hard. She just wanted me to get a job and get an education, and didn't see me going anywhere in athletics. I remember me and my brother was telling her that one day we're going to go to the Olympics. This will tell you how naïve my mom is, because she was like, "Well, okay, if you guys go, then I'll take the bus to come see you."'

Jackie paused long enough to laugh heartily along with me before continuing. 'Even after I had set the junior Olympic record in the pentathlon and was featured in *Sports Illustrated*'s "Faces in the Crowd" my mom was like, "What's going on here?" I will never forget. We had walked to the grocery store and they had my picture in the paper. The clerk was saying, "Oh, I've seen you." My mom was like, "What you in the paper for?" She thought I had gotten in trouble!'

Jackie would eventually be quoted as saying that 'the glory of sport comes from dedication, determination and desire. Achieving success and personal glory in athletics has less to do with wins and losses than it does with learning how to prepare yourself so that at the end of the day, whether on the track or in the office, you know that there was nothing more you could have done to reach your ultimate goal.'

GOLD RUSH

OLYMPIC SETBACK

My own chance for Olympic glory – or at least Olympic experience – first came in 1988, my second year of university, when I ran one of the fastest times in the world for the 200 metres and was an early favourite to be one of the top three in the country and make the Olympic team. In the qualifying round for the NCAA championships 200 metres later that year, I was running well and was one of the favourites to win. However, going around the bend I heard a pop first, then felt pain in my lower left leg. I stopped and couldn't put weight on it. I had suffered a stress fracture.

The Olympic trials were being held just six weeks from then, but I couldn't put a lot of weight on my leg, so I couldn't really train. Trying to recover as much from my disappointment as the injury, I worked out in the pool to remain in shape and finally got back on the track a couple of weeks before the trials. Although I knew it was going to be a little dicey, I still held out some hope that I had maintained enough conditioning to still make the team.

Although I had qualified for the trials in both the 200 and the 400, we decided that I would just run the 400 since the 400 put less strain on the leg. The pool workout, however, couldn't simulate working out on the track, and I had lost quite a bit of conditioning. I had tried to stay positive and maintain hope, but I just wasn't ready. I didn't advance out of the first round.

The year had been a breakthrough. I'd been riding really high. For the first time, I had felt certain that I could make the Olympic team and compete at that elite level. Now, suddenly, my dream had been crushed. My mother picked me up at the airport. On the way home she asked me about the experience. Unable to contain my disappointment any longer, I cried. I would be moved to tears again on the medal podium in Atlanta in 1996 after winning my first individual Olympic gold medal in the 400 metres.

3.

TECHNIQUE AND DNA

In sports requiring athletic movement, a huge part of the success of every world-class Olympic champion – including me – boils down to physicality and athleticism. As sports have become more and more popular, with increasing amounts of money being paid to the elite athletes, superior, God-given physical ability has become imperative. *Citius, Altius, Fortius*, the Olympic motto, explains it best. To win – or even compete – for Olympic medals, you have to be able to move faster, jump higher and be stronger than the rest of the field.

Unfortunately, a lack of real understanding about athleticism and biomechanics leads some athletes to believe that they really aren't athletically gifted. There is an assumption that anyone with athletic talent will be talented across the whole spectrum of athleticism, but that is not true. Plenty of people have athletic gifts in some areas but not in others.

I could easily say that I am not a naturally gifted athlete because I was terrible at basketball as a kid. I was pretty good on defence, but to this day I still miss getting the ball in the basket more often than I make it. Despite being 6'1" tall and a world-class athlete, I cannot dunk a basketball.

I'm also a lousy golfer. I first picked up a golf club 16 years ago. Over the years, even though I have never been a regular player and my play has always been sporadic and inconsistent, I have regularly committed myself to taking lessons and playing more often. Even so, I have failed to ever really improve. Friends and golf instructors tell me I must play more often than I do to better my game, but I have friends who don't play any more than I do and they have continued to improve, while I have not. This year it finally dawned on me that I lack the golf-related skills that come naturally to someone like Tiger Woods, who could then put in the work that has made him great. So I finally decided to quit trying and gave up a sport I have never really enjoyed anyway.

I'm just not great with most ball-related sports. A few years ago, I was at my best friend Ray Crockett's house. Ray was a star American football player and won two Superbowl rings with the Denver Broncos. His son Darryl, then four years old, and I were the only ones at the house. So when Darryl said he wanted to play catch, we got out the football and started throwing it back and forth a few times. Finally Darryl said, 'Throw it to *me*, Uncle Michael!' I had been trying to throw it to Darryl, but I was – and remain – an inferior ball thrower.

TECHNIQUE AND DNA

My obvious lack of ball-related talent could have led me to claim that I was an unlikely world-class athlete who became the fastest man in the world and a multiple Olympic champion solely because of my hard work. That would be a great story and very inspirational, especially since I did work extremely hard. But it wouldn't be completely true.

I simply have an aptitude for certain sports over others. I always knew, for example, that I would enjoy skiing, even though when I was growing up my parents could not have afforded to pay for me to participate in what is a very expensive sport. I had to wait to take up skiing, since I also couldn't take part while I was competing as a track athlete because of restrictions in my endorsement contracts. But the first chance I got after I retired, I put on skis for the first time while attending the Salt Lake City Winter Olympics in 2002. I took a two-hour lesson, and by the afternoon of that same day I was skiing on my own. The second time I skied I had advanced to intermediate-level slopes. Six years later, despite never taking another lesson and with just a few ski trips a year, I ski expert-level terrain and can confidently say that I am very good at it.

I'm just as naturally gifted when it comes to riding things on wheels. When I was a kid I loved riding both my skateboard and my bike. Two years ago I bought my son a skateboard and a ramp for his birthday. I had stopped riding skateboards when I was a young kid, probably at around 13 or 14, but when we headed outside to try it out I decided to get on. At 40 years old I discovered I could perform jumps and stunts that I had never tried before.

PHYSICAL GIFTS

In short, to be an Olympic champion you must have the superior athletic talent required for the sport you are participating in. The right body helps as well. Ian Thorpe wears a size 17 shoe, and Michael Phelps wears a size 14. In addition to this physical advantage, both these athletes have natural abilities superior to the average human that make them ideally suited to swimming. At the 2008 Beijing Olympics I watched Michael Phelps, who holds a staggering 16 Olympic medals including 14 golds, break records and demolish his competition, and make it look easy. Phelps, who is probably one of the most naturally gifted swimmers in history, was able to do things no one has ever done in swimming at the Olympic level.

Daley Thompson is one of the most physically talented people ever, a trait he wasn't reticent to acknowledge during our interview. 'I've met only a couple of people, Michael, that I feel were more physically talented or naturally gifted than I,' he said. Then he added, 'I've only met a couple of people who I feel probably worked harder than me. But I've never met anyone that I felt has both of those.'

He was so superior in part because he was a powerfully built athlete with perfect proportions. He's not too tall, he's not short, he's not too trim, he's not too big. He's the perfect size. When I look at Daley, I think of the sculpture of David. He's that kind of specimen.

Beyond his physicality, he possessed a trio of natural gifts. In most sports – whether it's soccer, basketball, baseball or the decathlon – you hear a lot of people talk about speed, which is important. You don't hear as much about strength, but that's equally important. Combine those two athletic attributes and you get explosive power – the ability to move quickly but with force. That's what Daley had. He wouldn't be the fastest and maybe not the strongest, but he is probably one of the most powerful athletes ever. And that advantage comes from his DNA. It's what made him so great.

Of course, that natural athleticism would never have been realised without his formidable work ethic. Daley wasn't much of a strategy type of guy. He was just a superior, hardworking, grind-it-out type of athlete. Ironically, he might have struggled had he competed in today's environment, because he lacked the technical component. Daley's attitude was: 'I'm physically prepared, I work hard, I can jump higher than you, I can run faster than you, now I'm just going to go out and beat you.' However, it's no longer enough to work hard and have superior athletic ability. To be in contention for medals nowadays, you have to be able to put those two together, but you also have to be technically sound. You have to understand your event and how to execute.

Before anything else, however, you have to make sure that you have the right body for the sport you've chosen. As a child Chris Hoy, five-time Olympic gold medallist and multiple world champion, attended a school that encouraged sports participation. 'I just used to love sport, any form of competition,' said Chris, now Sir Christopher, who is an ambassador to the London 2012 Olympics. 'I did rugby, I did track and field until age 17 and I did rowing.'

He was pretty good at all the sports he played, especially rowing, which he loved. 'The trouble with rowing is you're limited not by your physiology, but by your size. In rowing terms I'm pretty short at just 6'1". The best rowers in the world are 6'6" plus; they're big guys. I knew if I had any ambitions of taking rowing to a higher level, then I was going to have to be a lightweight rower. And even then I was going to be pretty short for that. But I was physically suited to cycling.' After racing around the world on the BMX circuit from age seven to 14, Chris transferred his skills to mountain biking, then road racing. 'Eventually, when I was about 17, I found the track. And I stuck with that. I think the first time you ride in a velodrome it's a whole new experience. You get bitten by the bug and you just want to do more of it.'

But don't rule out competing in a sport you love and you're good at just because your body doesn't look like those of most competitors in the sport. Many of Ian Thorpe's physical attributes could have been considered drawbacks. Instead of being tall and lean like most swimmers in the 2000 Sydney Olympics, he was tall and massive. 'I look like I should play football, but I'm in a pool,' Ian told me. Although his size provided benefits in terms of power, it also came with drawbacks. 'For me, although I have physical attributes that I can see lend themselves to some success, they also have a really high energy cost,' he said. So he focused on developing superior technique and made sure that he became 'the most efficient swimmer in the pool'.

TECHNIQUE AND DNA

MODUS OPERANDI

Athletes always have to deal with the balance between technique and athleticism. In many sports, like sprinting or golf, trying harder by using strength and power alone may actually cause an athlete to perform worse.

In sprinting, you want to develop strength and power. But they have to be developed in a particular way and for a specific purpose: not only to allow you as the athlete to generate more speed, but also to actually help you execute better technique. For example, as a 400-metre runner, I knew that the last 100 metres of that race would be the most difficult because of the toll that sprinting the first 300 metres would take. The 400-metre race is a very long sprint, so the final 100 metres I'm in what is called fatigue mode, where my body is tired and wants nothing more than for me to stop pushing it to sprint. The way to train for this particularly important phase of the race is to first focus on technique. Proper, efficient sprinting technique is important in all phases of the race, but nowhere in a 400 are you more vulnerable to sloppy or inefficient technique than the last 100 metres. So my objective was always to minimise the differential in stride length and stride frequency between the non-fatigue stage of the race, or the first 200 metres, and the fatigue stage of the race.

The best way to control the efficiency of the technique during that fatigue mode is to develop good upper-body strength. This often comes as a surprise to people, because they don't understand what arm strength has to do with sprinting and certainly can't understand what having good shoulder strength has to do with leg stride frequency. The arms drive the legs, and when that arm strength starts to go because of fatigue over the last 100 metres, the arms don't swing with the same power or velocity as they can, and the legs, which are already heavy from fatigue themselves, respond to what the arms do. To counter this issue, my strength coach and I developed a programme that included developing the shoulder, chest, bicep, triceps, deltoid and trapezoid muscles – all muscles related to the arm, shoulder, neck and torso area. Some of these muscles are directly related to arm strength and velocity, and some are muscles that support those primary muscles. After I started on this strength programme in the off season prior to the 1993 season, I improved my personal best by two tenths of a second and ran 43 seconds three times that year, a feat I had only accomplished once in the previous three years of my professional career.

This was a result of working with my coach, Clyde, and my strength coach Danny Brabham, taking the feedback from what Clyde was seeing during my races. Video analysis showed a significant breakdown in technique during the fatigue phase of the race whenever I really pushed the front part of the race. We knew that in order to run faster times I would have to push the pace of the front part of the race but couldn't afford a breakdown in technique on the back end of the race. So we worked with Danny and explained what type of strength I would need and where I would need that strength in order to combat the upper-body muscle fatigue at the end of the race and avoid a breakdown of technique.

TECHNIQUE AND DNA

ATHLETES, TECHNICIANS OR BOTH?

Some sports are more technique based and some are more physical. And some Olympic events involve so much technique and so little physicality that some question whether they're really sports at all. This argument has become particularly heated over the last several years while, in an effort to remain modern and current and to maintain and grow its fan base, the IOC has added new Olympic events, including trampoline and bowling. But are all these new events sports?

I would argue yes. All of the events in the Olympics where individuals or teams are competing against one another are sports. The mix-up comes when people automatically assume that if something is a sport, the participants must be athletes, and that's not true.

Sport is about competition and anyone can compete, whether they are athletes or not. But not all sportspeople are athletes. All Olympians aren't athletes. This sometimes offends the people taking part in some of these sports, but my position is not meant to offend. I just don't believe that the individuals taking part in sports like archery or shooting are athletes. I believe the Olympic motto of 'Stronger, Higher, Faster' sums up the requirements for sports participants to be considered athletes.

While an archer or a shooter isn't an athlete in my opinion, that doesn't mean he or she is any less skilled or works any less hard than athletes. In many ways I have tremendous respect and admiration for participants in sports like these that are so heavily skill based. In my own sport of athletics, even as a sprinter where races are won and lost by hundredths of a second, if I place my foot just slightly outside the area where it should land on a step it is not going to make a huge difference to the outcome of the race. Quite the contrary for an archer or a shooter. The skill and muscle memory that are required, and the consistency that is needed in their movement, are things I only wish that I could duplicate. Just the slightest millimetre off in movement or technique can cost the participant a medal. The years and hours of training that it takes to perfect this technique require no less commitment and no less focus than it did for me to win gold medals in my sport. So while they may not be athletes, they are incredible technicians.

By definition, a technician is going to focus almost exclusively on technique. That's not as clear when it comes to athletes, who need both technique and power. Even though the argument is always about whether an athlete should place more focus on technique or physical training, the issue is really at what stage in an athlete's development and at what stage in an athlete's training cycle should you place more focus on technique rather than physical training. At Michael Johnson Performance we have found that the early stages of an athlete's development – the years between the ages of 12 and 15 – are the prime physical development years. These are the years when an athlete's body goes through its natural changes and development, and also when it is ripe for physical development. However, most parents helping their kids and most coaches working with kids tend to focus mostly on skill during that period, figuring that the athlete's physical development isn't as important because the athlete has the speed, power and strength that he has and there is no real improvement to be had here. That is simply not true. And it's a shame, because in many cases the focus placed on skill and technique to the detriment of physicality deprives athletes of reaching their full potential in their sport.

SUPER-SIZE ABILITY

As Chris Hoy and Ian Thorpe would discover, magic can happen when DNA dovetails with natural aptitude and honed technique. But there are different levels of ability even at the highest level of sports, and those differences, even at their most subtle, make huge differences at the Olympic level.

Tyson Gay is one of the greatest sprinters of all time. He is a world champion at both 100 metres and 200 metres. He is the American record holder at 100 metres. When he gets into his running, his turnover, the simple ability to pick his legs up and put them down, is unmatched by anyone else currently and possibly in history. He is not the greatest starter in the business, but he has such superior natural turnover that he can overcome his poor start, catch the other athletes, and still pull out victories. He is a great 200-metre runner, one of the best ever. He has also run 44 seconds for 400 metres, which means he has a unique combination of speed and strength and speed endurance – the ability to hold significant speed for a long time – relative to the sprint races.

Despite all that, Tyson Gay will probably never win another World Championship gold medal or ever win an Olympic gold medal in the 100 or 200 metres, because in 2008, the year after Gay won double gold in the 100 and 200 at the World Championships in Osaka, Usain Bolt came on the scene and started to rewrite the history books by doing things no one had ever done before in the history of the sport.

I was working as an expert analyst for the BBC on 16 August 2008, the day that history was made and the world was struck by a bolt of lightning. And even though I had spent my life running fast and helping others to run fast, Usain blew my mind by running faster than anyone thought possible. How had he managed to redefine the limits of how fast we can go? The answer lies, in part, in Usain's physicality.

Usain, who is 6'5" and one of the most gifted athletes ever in the history not only of athletics but of sport in general, has a unique ability to take that height and execute a sprint previously thought to be more suited to an athlete 5'10" to 6' tall. Traditionally, athletes of his height are unable to turn those long limbs over quickly enough to generate the quickness required over such a short sprint, and therefore cannot take advantage of having a longer stride than the competition. Usain, however, manages to cycle his legs in order to take full advantage of his longer stride without those long legs having a negative impact at the start of the race, when the shorter athletes would normally have an advantage. Somehow he has no difficulty unfolding his long legs out of the start position and quickly driving out of the blocks.

Over history, 100-metre champions like Carl Lewis and Linford Christie were taller than the average sprinter and they were almost always at the back of the pack at the start of the race. Not until they could get out of the drive phase, which takes place in the first 30 or so metres, would they be able to get into their long stride and pull out the victory in the second part of the race. Usain Bolt is so much better because he doesn't have to wait that long. He has either the natural ability, or he has figured out how, to start and execute the drive phase of the race like an athlete much shorter than he is. He gives up very little if anything to his competitors at the start of the race, so by the time they've all gone through the drive phase he is even with them. Then, in very short order, he is able to put significant distance between himself and the field.

Ironically, like so many Olympic champions, Usain didn't start off thinking that he would focus on the sport that eventually made him famous. As a kid he was simply so active – playing and climbing on everything – that in self-defence his parents gave him housework to do in the mornings to keep him occupied. Tanni Grey-Thompson, who was born with spina bifida and competed in a wheelchair, says her parents got her into sports for the same reason. 'I had way too much energy and was probably a bit annoying,' she says. 'So I think they thought the more sports I did, [the more] it might tire me out.' That echoed history-making gymnast Nadia Comaneci's experience. She had so much energy that she kept jumping up and down on everything she could find, including the sofa, and her mother finally enrolled her in gymnastics. The decision, of course, would shape her life.

In Usain's case, however, the man who would redefine sprinting didn't stumble on to running right away. 'I was a cricket lover all my life, so for me it was all about cricket. Then all of the sudden I'm a track star.' Once Usain committed to sprinting, he wrapped his long arms around the concept, including those events he supposedly wasn't physically suited for. 'He surprised me,' admits Usain's father Wellesley, who was also known as a fast runner in his youth. 'The 200 was where I thought he would do well. For the 100, that was a shock to me. I always said, "You're too tall. They're going to leave you in the blocks." He said, "Daddy, I am running, not you." That's what he said! "I am the one running, not you."'

I first heard about Usain back in 2000. Jamaica has produced many a great sprinter, so when you hear of a teenager from that island running great times and winning junior championships, you take notice. At just 15 and already 6'2", he was making his name as a runner at 200 and 400 metres – my distances.

HOW LOW CAN YOU GO?
A decade after Usain first walked through the gates of William Knibb School, he entered Beijing's Bird's Nest stadium in 2008 to run the race of his life. Driven as much

by a desire not to lose as by his grandmother's admonition to 'Go over there and do your best, and whatever you do, you'll satisfy,' he broke the world record not once, but twice. His astounding performance reopened one of mankind's oldest questions: how fast can a man run? For a century, the world record for the 100 metres has been the measure. One hundred years before Usain's historic race in Beijing, the record stood at 10.6 seconds.

At the Berlin Olympic Games, my hero, the great Jesse Owens, ran a time of 10.2 seconds: a world record that would stand for over 20 years. Germany's Armin Harry reignited the whole debate about the limits of human speed when he ran 10 seconds flat in 1960. Suddenly it seemed that running 100 metres faster than 10 seconds might be possible. But the world would have to wait another eight years until the 1968 Olympic Games in Mexico. High altitude and thin air helped athletes push the boundaries, and Jim Hines won the 100 metres in 9.95 seconds.

The 10-second barrier had been breached. Hines's win would be the most talked about 100 metres until Canadian Ben Johnson's at the Seoul Olympics in 1988. Unfortunately for the sport, Johnson's urine sample, collected on Saturday 24 September 1988 after Johnson had set a new world record of 9.79 seconds and apparently won gold, was found to contain the metabolates of a banned substance: an anabolic steroid called Stanozolol.

For those who believed that such astonishing times were beyond natural human physiology, this was all the proof they needed. Rightly or wrongly, no 100-metre world record would ever be viewed without suspicion again. It would be over a decade before Maurice Greene matched Ben's mark of 9.79. In doing so, he became the 14th man to officially hold the 100-metre world record. Six years later, in 2005, a small island in the Caribbean Sea laid claim to having the world's fastest man, Asafa Powell. By 2007 this quiet Jamaican had lowered the mark to an astonishing 9.74 seconds. Perhaps the success of his compatriot is what persuaded Usain to start experimenting with the 100 metres.

Much has changed in track and field since Donald Lippincott ran 10.6 seconds for the 100 metres in 1912, including the starting blocks, the track, timing methods, footwear, training techniques and nutrition. Physically, meanwhile, a man is much the same now as he was a century ago. In Beijing, Usain Bolt ran a second faster than Lippincott, and he could clearly go even faster. After setting a 100-metre world record of 9.69 seconds, he broke his own record by over one tenth of a second.

I met Usain in Kingston after visiting with his parents in Usain's home town of Trelawny, a rural parish three hours' drive from the capital across Jamaica's Blue Mountains. A year after Usain had stunned the world with his mind-boggling Olympic double gold, the first question he asked was whether I missed competing now that I was retired. 'I just want to relax,' he said. 'I don't think I'm going to miss track, because it's hard. It's hard work.'

Usain may already be anticipating being able to put his feet up when he retires, but for me, I never managed to slow down – not entirely. Back home in Dallas, where I grew up,

TECHNIQUE AND DNA

I'm dedicating my time to helping others achieve their athletic dreams through my performance centre. Some of the best athletes in the world come to Michael Johnson Performance to learn how to run faster, get stronger, and improve all facets of their athletic performance.

Since Usain Bolt's speeds, we've been a whole lot busier. He's inspired people all over the world. The people who come to me want to learn from the best, and I guess my achievements and a life at the pinnacle of track and field make me that man. Now that my days of winning gold medals are over for me, the laps around the track have been replaced by the laptop. But the philosophy that moulded my own athletic career has stayed the same.

PERFECTING PERFORMANCE

Now more than ever, I believe that running fast is more than just a God-given talent. It's a skill that can be perfected by coaching and the application of good technique. That belief is the cornerstone of my performance centre. Paula Radcliffe holds the world record in the women's marathon but knows that improved flat speed can make all the difference at the next Olympic Games. That's why she comes to me. The same goes for guys hoping to become the next multi-million-dollar stars in the NFL, where speed is one of the most prized assets. They've come here to get faster, ahead of the NFL Combine, a test that could change their lives. Arsenal Football Club send their Academy athletes to us. The UK Bobsleigh team also attends training camps organised by

Michael Johnson Performance. Like Paula, their bodies are already well tuned for the task at hand. They come here to improve their technique.

This place is as much a lab as a gym. We humans don't think of ourselves as machines, but in many ways that is how we perform, how we move. Biomechanics is a science that applies mechanical principles to the human body. For sprint coaches, that science is a vital tool for perfecting technique, because to run really fast, technique is crucial. Efficiency makes you faster.

When I run, for example, other than my arms, you don't see any movement in the torso. Ironically, when I started getting recruited by different colleges, some of the coaches said, 'Hey, you're going to have to change your style.' I had always been a little bit more upright than the others, and some of the kids, including my friends, would make fun of my running stance. But I was faster than they were, so eventually some of them began to try to run like me, even if I did 'run funny'.

Still, when a variety of coaches told me I would have to change, I just figured, 'Well, that's part of what I am going to have to do to improve. Great, fine, not a problem.' Luckily, the coach I ultimately chose, Clyde Hart, never said anything about changing my upright running style. Instead, we worked on improving technique, including correcting the habit I had of throwing my head up when I got fatigued, which would make me even more upright.

By 1990, when I started to get all of this focus and attention from the sports media, the television commentators began to talk about how different my upright style was and said that if I leaned more as I ran I'd be able to break the world record. That became a huge subject of discussion. Ironically, it turned out that my style was actually much more efficient than everyone else's.

Being upright gave me the ability to produce much more power than some of my competitors or than the typical sprinter. I was naturally blessed with more fast-twitch muscle fibres and so therefore speed than the average person. Beyond that, from a physical standpoint, my body is such that I can consistently lift weights and I would never get really big. I could lift large amounts of weight and I had very good strength at my peak as an athlete, but you didn't see it and I didn't have to carry the extra weight around. It was like having the power of an 18-wheeler in the body of a Ferrari. That was an advantage, because as a sprinter you need to lift for strength but you don't want to get too bulky, which compromises flexibility, along with fluidity and technical soundness. But if I hadn't learned how to drive it correctly, my Ferrari body might as well have been a VW Beetle.

Technique is extremely important as a sprinter and, as I noted previously, a lot of it boils down to how efficiently you move. Just imagine looking from above at a sprinter in action. Do you see one foot land within the plane of his body and then the other foot land in front of his body as well? That's good, efficient technique. If one foot lands out to the right of his body, the next foot is going to land out to his left, and then he's zigzagging down the track, however slightly, as opposed to straight. As small as those little differences are, that zigzag will cost a competitor a couple of centimetres with each step since the foot went the same distance but landed outside to the right and then outside to the left. That makes a big difference ultimately.

As a runner, how you use your upper body is equally important. The legs are like the engine that runs your body. In your car you've got an engine but you don't crank the engine; you don't turn that engine with your hand. You use an accelerator. Your arms are like the accelerator. They drive your legs. They also determine the efficiency of your legs.

So now if you're looking at a sprinter running directly at you down the track with his arms pumping up and down, you should see each hand coming up just to the side of his head or right in front of his nose. If one hand comes across his shoulder, then the other is going to come back across the other shoulder the other way and that's going to pull his body over that way. If his right arm goes all the way across his body to his left shoulder as it goes up and down, that's going to pull his body to the left. The other side is going to go back the opposite way and pull to the right. That will cause the same zigzag movement down the track that was visible in the bird's eye view.

For the movement to be efficient, you want the arms to come across no further than the midline of the body. If they don't come up to your nose and instead go over to your shoulder, that's too far. Which brings us back to physicality. If you got really bulky and put on too much weight in your shoulders and arms, all that muscle would make it hard to keep that arm going up and down in a straight line and not cross the midline.

For every Olympic sport there is a set of techniques that produce the most efficient and powerful movement, and there are body types that will work best within those parameters. The same applies for the different specialities within that sport. I can look at an athlete doing a general workout and I can tell you from his physical build whether he's more suited for 100 metres, 200 metres or 400 metres. They're all sprints, but each demands different levels of quickness, speed endurance (how long they can run fast) and endurance (how long they can last, period).

Although many thought my running style was unusual, it incorporated method and technique. The strides were not short, as many had thought. In fact most people only assumed this because my superior and very quick turnover gave the illusion of a shorter stride. I had great leg speed. There was economy of movement and speed aiding the speed endurance central for 200 and 400 metres. That relaxed, upright posture – shoulders in line, head still – meant I was able to flow along the track.

Coach and I worked with the US Olympic Committee (USOC), who had footage of me and the technology to analyse my running technique and mechanics. The USOC created a model for ideal sprint technique, and when my technique was plugged in against the model, I outran the model. What we found from this analysis disproved a couple of different assumptions about my technique that had been talked about repeatedly by the commentators and sports writers as well as other coaches. The first was that my stride was short, and the other was that my knee lift was low. Neither was true.

I was relieved when Coach and I discovered that my running style was actually a benefit. Previously we had received a lot of criticism for not changing my style. We always took the approach that we didn't see that my style was creating any negative effect, so we saw no reason to change it just because it wasn't like other people's running style. We tried to explain it, but to most people it didn't make any sense. All they knew was that my style was different from what they were accustomed to seeing and different from what the other sprinters were doing; so, in their simple logic, I had to be the one who was wrong. Now we had an answer for all those critics who kept saying that I could break the world record if I only changed my running style.

We knew all along that it didn't make sense to change my natural style just because people said I should or because everyone else sprinted differently. Having proof of that made us feel really good. Even better, during the two days we spent looking at the information and analysing the findings, we learned that not only was my stride length and knee lift within the normal range, but also my more upright posture was actually helping me to generate more power and quicker turnover. My more upright position puts my upper body and torso over my hips, which allows me to generate a larger amount of downforce with each step. Downforce is power, and power is speed. The greater the force that each step strikes the ground with, the faster you run. Being able to create more power and strike the ground with more force helped me to run faster. Additionally, being more upright while sprinting allows each foot as it goes through its cycle to generate a tighter cycle. A tighter cycle is a faster cycle. The more forward lean you have, the longer the trip your trail leg must make around the cycle. The trail leg is the leg that has just struck the ground and is in the process of recovering or cycling around while the other leg is making ground contact.

We didn't just stop with that. We developed training to enhance my style and continued throughout my career to improve on the efficiency of my sprint style.

My style, however, was never ideal over the shortest of sprints, the 100 metres. My biggest advantages over the longer sprints, speed endurance and efficiency, are not major advantages for the 100-metre sprint. We like to talk about the 100 metres as being in phases. The explosive start is followed by the drive phase. In the start, keeping low, head down, allows the build-up of speed, pushing off the track with the toes, arms pumping back and forth, using that upper-body strength. It's all about acceleration. In the drive phase you're approaching maximum velocity. Head in line with the spine, relaxed, elbows at 90 degrees, stride extended, classic high-knee lift. If it's close, you'll need to lean for the line.

Sprinters who race the 100 metres are powerful, of course, and generally not too tall. The shorter you are, the more compact you are and the lower your centre of gravity. Of course, you don't want to be too short, since a good stride length is an advantage in that final sprint for the line. In general, however, height much over 6' has long been regarded as a major disadvantage in the early phases of the race. Tall guys with long legs like Usain, who is 6'5", have a very difficult time getting out of the blocks and into that drive phase. Keeping a low centre of gravity is equally challenging. That's why Usain's father was so surprised that his son wanted to compete in the 100 metres, and why even Usain's coaches didn't initially believe that he had prospects as a 100-metre runner despite his natural speed. But Usain knew better.

Like me, Usain realised he was physically gifted as a kid. Like me, he was just faster than everyone else. 'I was always doing great things,' Usain told me. 'When I started track and field, I was good naturally. Even in high school, I didn't train and I was always running fast times and breaking records. It's just a talent. God put everybody on this earth to do something. This is for me. I'm just doing my part right now.'

Usain's freakish speed allows him to achieve results that defy logic. Those are things you cannot teach, so it's no surprise to me that he puts his speed down to the Almighty. To be fair, he hasn't just relied on his superior physicality and natural talent. He's worked on his start, and at 25 he now has the power required for this explosive part of the race.

'Can Bolt be faster?' everyone asks. Absolutely. Having studied his technique – or lack thereof – I know this unequivocally. His lateral movement is horrible as he gets out and up into his maximum velocity. During a race his thigh actually points into his competitor's lane, so the force that he is driving through is actually coming out at an oblique angle instead of right down the track. In order to compensate for that, he now has to do some side bending and some de-rotation up above, so that he doesn't get pulled off into the lane next to him. He also gets a lot of sway in his shoulder motion. You want some rotation but you want it to be stabilised. What you're seeing is some side bending. Each time the side of his body collapses, he has to actually strike and recover. That causes him to lose a lot of time.

When I asked Usain about his weaknesses, he confided that he feels he still needs to work on making his starts consistent. And he doesn't think that he's fully perfected his last 30 metres in the 200-metre race. 'I notice sometimes I start reaching. I'm trying to get to the line so much I start reaching too early,' he says.

It's almost scary to think about how fast Usain could go if he cleaned up some of his running and brought his technique up to the level of his congenital gift. Regardless of the sport and whether it requires natural athletic ability or natural skill or a combination of both, I don't believe that anyone can achieve Olympic success, competing against the best in the world, without having that kind of natural superior talent. It is easier for a sportsperson in a skill-based sport to achieve success through repetition and early adaptation than it would be for someone to gain athletic ability through repetition. I think it is virtually impossible for someone to develop superior athleticism through training and repetition. In my opinion, athletes can often develop a certain skill through repetition, but probably not enough to be the best in the world.

On the other hand, some Olympic athletes have proved me wrong and actually overcome what they or others perceive as a lack of raw, physical talent by perfecting their technique.

TECHNICAL SUCCESS

'So many people told me when I was growing up that I'd never make a good swimmer,' double gold medal holder Rebecca Adlington told me. 'So many people said I kicked way too much for a distance swimmer.' Rebecca, who describes herself as 'very big ... and not the leanest of girls', not only chose to ignore them, she went on to prove them wrong, even though she was 'rubbish in the gym', with her shoulders giving way when she lifted weights of any significance. 'I can't actually do it,' she said. 'Yet, put me in a pool and I would keep going all day and I don't ever find it a problem. I think, technically, how my muscles work in the pool is so different to anything else.' So even though Rebecca's raw physical talent may not be as strong as some other great swimmers, her technique coupled with her mental strength gives her an advantage that often proves unbeatable.

That's why she and her coach Bill Furniss focus so intently on perfecting how she moves in the water, starting with her position in the water, which is higher than most. 'It's always been a thing for me that if my technique's not right, I don't swim well. That's why I'm so glad I've stayed with the same coach since such an early age, because he knows exactly what to look for. He knows that I've got to keep my stroke at a certain length for the first 150 metres of my race. If I shorten it, I won't have a good race because I can't get into a rhythm.

'Getting my stroke right is something we always focused on. My coach is 57, so he's pretty old school in how he coaches. With swimming now, everybody wants to try loads of different stuff on land, and film, and do all this technical stuff. My coach says, "No, do the work in the pool and it'll pay off. It's the work in the pool that matters." Over the years he's always been strict with his swimmers, including me, about having good technique. As soon as he notices your technique going, he'll say, "I don't care if your times aren't quick. Hold your stroke."'

You'll find that same emphasis on technique in many an Olympic champion's story. Technique was emphasised so early on in Nadia Comaneci's career that she never had a chance to develop bad habits. 'The base of gymnastics has to be really clean and technically correct,' she explained. 'Every skill has to be learned the right way, otherwise you cannot build on more difficult moves.' That wasn't an issue for Nadia, who at the age of 14 would earn the first perfect 10 ever awarded to a gymnast for her routine on the uneven bars. Nadia, who was already known for her performance of innovative and challenging skills, would add another six perfect 10s during those 1976 Olympics Games. Even later in life, Nadia's execution and technique remained flawless. 'I remember at one point, even after so many years, my coach Béla Károlyi's wife Marta – who coaches the US team now – said, "Nadia doesn't know how to do a move incorrectly because she hasn't learned how to do it incorrectly."' What Marta meant was that Nadia didn't know how to bend in certain moves where that would cause a deduction, for example, because she had learned to do those moves with straight legs.

Few athletes think about technique when they're young. Nadia's five golds and Rebecca's self-evaluation, along with her record, show us what a mistake that is. However, even the most perfectly suited physicality and perfectly executed technique aren't enough. You have to want to make Olympic history deep down in your core. You have to be willing to do whatever it takes.

4.

DOING WHAT IT
TAKES TO WIN

Without the right DNA, the gift of natural ability and solid technique, you won't be successful as an Olympic athlete. But that's just the start. Next comes the work, which is driven by commitment and dedication to the gruelling training sessions in the weight room and on the track, on the court or field or in the pool. Olympic athletes in general, and especially those who rise to the top, don't just commit to becoming Olympic champions or to competing at the Olympic Games. Nor do they simply commit themselves to the glory and reward of winning or accomplishing their goals. Those commitments are easy. They don't even just say they will work hard and sweat, and go through pain and sacrifice. They commit to consistently doing what they know it will take to be their absolute best day to day and even hour to hour.

The desire to succeed is extremely important, but it's easy to want to be the best in the world. Drive is more important. It's easy to commit to being the Olympic gold medallist, but not as easy to commit to training 50 per cent harder than you did the year before and to making sacrifices to achieve that goal. It is that drive that causes an individual to work for what he desires.

'I never felt I'd done enough or gone quick enough,' says Tanni Grey-Thompson. 'So I was quite driven and quite focused. It was never a problem to make myself go out and train. You could probably count on one hand the number of times in all the years that it was like, "I just can't do that" [because of fatigue or injury].'

The training required to compete at the championship level Tanni demanded of herself meant that everything else in her life took a back seat. And I mean everything. In 2001, when she and her husband decided to have a family, they actually got out the calendar. The next Games were in 2002. When they worked back, they realised that if Tanni was to regain her fitness in time after her pregnancy, 'We were going to have a family right *then*.' So they started trying straight away.

Somehow, having competition dictate the rest of life seemed perfectly normal to Tanni. 'It never felt too intrusive. It was just always what I wanted to do more than anything else,' she told me. 'I was lucky my parents and my family really understood that, so they put up with lots of me not being there for Christmas or training on Christmas, birthdays or anniversaries. It was fine. I set my wedding date based on my competition schedule. My sister set her wedding on my competition schedule. When she decided to get married, she sat down and said, "Right, okay, you need to be at the wedding. What date is going to work for you?" It was really nice that she wanted me to be at the wedding and she wasn't saying, "We're getting married in the summer." She was like, "You're not going to be around in the summer. We'll get married in February."

Tanni's life revolved around racing, and those close to her not only understood, they supported that, especially Ian, her husband, who was also her coach. 'Ian, for one of my birthdays, bought me some aluminium from Russia to build a racing chair. I remember a friend saying, "Oh my God, you were so good at pretending that's what you really wanted for your birthday."' Tanni answered, 'No, that's really what I wanted for my birthday.'

Athletes like Tanni who have the incredible drive and single-minded focus required to become Olympic champions don't let obstacles and setbacks get in their way. It's not as simple as saying, 'I'm not going to let that particular setback or obstacle affect me.' It means figuring out a way around the obstacle.

When I was competing I never lacked for motivation to go out to the track and train every day, even when temperatures were over 100 degrees for more than 30 straight days, as they were in 1994. Most world-class athletes don't have a problem with training each day. They understand that training makes them better and gets them closer to accomplishing their goal. The pivotal point in most Olympic champions' lives is that moment when desire for Olympic victory meets the willingness to commit at that level and to that degree.

In my third year of college, after not making the 1988 Olympic team, my indoor track season started with a bang. I won my first NCAA championship and set a new American record in the 200 metres in the process. I also finished second at the US senior indoor championships in the 400 metres. Due to a lack of focus, I hadn't been running as well during my outdoor season when I pulled my quadriceps in the 100 metres at the conference championships. I found myself rehabbing again, unable to run at the NCAA outdoor championships. So I was shocked to get the opportunity to go to Europe and run races that summer of 1989.

I didn't turn in a great performance in my races abroad. Even so, the experience would change my life. During my month in Europe I was exposed to what professional track and field is all about. I saw all the top athletes compete, including Carl Lewis, Jackie Joyner-Kersee and Sergey Bubka. I watched Roger Kingdom break the 110 metres hurdles world record. I remember being in the hotel hanging out with some friends not too far away from Kingdom, along with his agent and a group of people who treated him like a superstar. I'd heard already that he'd made a lot of money for breaking that world record.

On the long plane ride home, all I could think about was what I had seen in Europe and the possibility of competing professionally at that level. I knew that I would need to remain healthy to have any chance at all of reaching that goal. I called my coach and asked him to meet me. 'I know

I'm not doing as much as I should on the stretching front and in my strength-training sessions,' I admitted. 'I'll do whatever I need to in order to finish the season healthy.'

I committed to stretching as much as necessary and to lifting weights with the same commitment and intensity that I put into the daily track training that I loved so much. To further minimise the risk of injury, Coach decided that I would run only 400-metre races and relays all season. It worked.

I would venture to say that most if not all Olympic champions have experienced that moment where desire to be the best, the realisation of what it will take and the willingness to put in the effort all merge. Soon after Sally Gunnell focused in on the 400 metres hurdles to the exclusion of other track events she had dabbled with early in her career, she developed the drive required to cross the finish line first. Although she had experienced early success in the Olympics and elsewhere, a four-year dry spell followed. Then she came in fifth in a close race. 'That was probably the first time I thought I had a chance to win in four years' time. What it made me realise is that I loved what I was doing.' It also made her hungry. 'It made me realise, you know what, this is what I really want in life.' That gave her back the focus she needed. Just as importantly, it helped her understand that she needed to approach her sport more professionally and get the help she needed with both mechanics and injury prevention.

IN GOOD HEALTH AND BAD

Part of being an athlete is dealing with injuries, which are major setbacks and very difficult mentally to get through. Not only does an injury stop the athlete from being able to compete, the very reason we train in the first place, but it stops all progress towards the goal which is the prize. Worse, it actually destroys some of that progress. After an injury, the athlete, who has been working towards a goal and using that goal as a motivator and a focus in training each day, has to make an adjustment. Instead of training his body to accomplish the goal, which he had been doing to this point, he now has to heal his body before he can go back to training his body. The healing process for a world-class athlete usually consists of a combination of rehabilitation exercises and rest. Both of those activities run exactly counter to what the athlete wants to do and what he was doing before the injury. Rehab exercises are like taking a highly trained physicist and making him do simple arithmetic exercises every day. They are tedious, simple and significantly below the athlete's normal capabilities. Resting is extremely important to heal an injury, but you can't really put any effort into resting. It is a passive activity.

This is where drive becomes really important. During the difficult period of time required for rehab and rest to heal an injury, the athlete with superior drive will put the same energy, effort and focus required into his rehab as he did into training. Yes, it is difficult to dedicate the same energy and effort and commitment to simple exercises that aren't making you a better athlete but are only making it possible for you to get back to a state where you can start to work again at becoming a better athlete. And yes, it takes significant drive and focus on the overall goal to resist starting back to training too soon instead of being patient and resting.

It is at this time in fact that athletes are most vulnerable to losing focus on their goal and becoming distracted. With more time on their hands than they're used to, they sometimes fall into a pattern of hanging out with friends more, drinking more, partying more, or indulging in some other pattern of activity that replaces the satisfaction they previously got from training towards their goal. It takes serious drive to sit in your house every day and stay on the same disciplined schedule you were on before the injury, when now you're not getting closer to your goal and are bored to death.

In rare cases, however, an athlete manages not only to overcome an injury, but to turn it into an asset. How Ian Thorpe dealt with his broken ankle just ten months before the 2000 Sydney Olympics reveals both pragmatism and mental strength. With the exception of the first few days, Ian's post-injury course of action could serve as a lesson for any injured athlete. I'll let Ian, who was just 16 at the time of the injury, share his experience in his own words.

'I was running through a national park and I trod on an uneven rock, triangular shaped. I can remember feeling it and thinking, "Whoah, that hurt." I started to walk, but that hurt more and I wanted to get back to the pool as quickly as I could, so I jogged back to the pool. My ankle was broken and swollen at this stage, but I couldn't see because the swelling was in my shoe. I got back to the pool and, totally by chance, the best swimming physiotherapist was at the pool that afternoon. I told him what happened and, after a very brief look at it, he said, "It's pretty much fine." (I still bring this up all the time when I see him.) When I took my shoe off, however, it completely ballooned.

'My reaction to it was not that I'm in pain. It was straight into the process of okay, I've got an injury; I have to get rid of it. So I started swimming and doing a little kick swimming. I figured that would probably get some of the fluid from around my ankle away. I didn't do well in the session but I got through it. I then swum the next day, two swim sessions. It was certainly hurting a bit to walk, but I got through the next day. The following day I trained in the morning. Then I had to take a helicopter to get to an appearance I was doing. By then my ankle was so swollen I couldn't wear shoes, so I was wearing a pair of slides, you know, like flip-flops.

'Even though I still didn't think it was anything serious, I decided then it was probably a good idea to get an X-ray. Then, since training was coming up, I left for the pool before getting the results, which were sent to my doctor. It turns out that I had actually snapped my ankle in half. My doctor called my mother, who then came to the pool. Suddenly my coach was screaming at me: "Get out!"

'I didn't know what was wrong. What was I doing wrong in the session?

'I can remember my mum gave me the kind of look that says that fate had just struck one of those blows that you can't contend with and started to cry. I looked at her and I wasn't willing to accept that this was a time for tears. This wasn't the end of my preparation for the Olympics.

'I had it cast that afternoon. I chose a fibreglass cast, which weighed a ton but would allow me to still do some swimming. I took two days off, maybe three, but I got back in the pool and started training. I knew my legs were great. I had a reputation for having such a strong kick. Now I had to start using my upper body a little bit more. I realised that my broken ankle could be an opportunity to start working on something new and getting me out of my comfort zone. Building my upper-body strength became the next part of the Olympic preparation. I started to become muscular through my upper body and torso, because of what I was dragging behind me. Basically I began to transition physically from a boy to a man during that time.'

Once Ian's ankle had healed, he still had to contend with the muscle loss in the leg that had been immobilised in a cast. 'Even two years after the Games, my legs were still uneven,' he said. Even so, the only doubt he had about competing was the very first session after the cast had come off and he had been cleared to return to regular training. 'You'll be right to do what you want now. Just be cautious,' he was told. In that first session, however, 'I wasn't at my best,' says Ian. 'In my mind at that stage, it clicked into, "Oh, maybe this is a bigger problem than you've given this credit for." But I only thought that way for one session.

After that, it was time to move on and do everything, so I didn't think like that again.'

WORK ETHIC

Some athletes, like Rebecca Adlington and Chris Hoy, are about to inspire a future generation as much with their work ethic as with their performance. In 2006 Rebecca had to deal with her sister's hospitalisation and being ill herself. 'I still managed to come out of it and go on to the Olympics [two years later] and do well,' she told me. 'A girl [in my little swimming club] is going through exactly the same thing at the minute. She's always asking, "How long did it take you?" "Did you find this?" I really like the fact that people feel like they can come up to me and ask me that sort of stuff. Apart from the home Olympics, I've pretty much been through most things in my career. I would always want to pass down my advice. I'm not saying it's the right thing to do. It's just my advice and what I would do or what I did. And because I do everything properly and demand 100 per cent from myself every time I'm in the pool, it's made people realise, "If I do it properly, maybe I would get to her level." I think that's the biggest thing I pass on in my club.'

Chris Hoy is another athlete to emulate. Whether or not he wins a single medal in the London 2012 Games, let alone the three golds he's shooting for, he represents the highest Olympic standard. Despite the lack of coaches, champions to emulate and money of any kind until the late nineties, when the UK's National Lottery began providing funding for the top few athletes in the country, he devoted 100 per cent of his natural talent and effort to his sport of choice. 'I'd finished university in 1999, and I went straight from being a full-time student into being a full-time athlete,' Chris told me. 'At that point I still didn't necessarily believe that I would be an Olympic champion. In fact, it would have been a ridiculous idea at the time to think that I could have done that. It was so far off from where I was. But my personal goal was just to see how far I could go and to keep improving. I was not really worried too much about the outcome. Just keep taking steps forward. From there on, it was one more step at a time. When I made the next step, that became my new point for starting from. I just kept looking for ways to get better.

'I'm quite stubborn and determined. If I set myself a goal or a challenge, I will keep working on it. All the years I've been competing at different sports, there have always been guys that you would have put money on becoming really talented, captain of the Scottish rugby team or winning a medal in whatever sport in the Olympics. You'd see these guys who could do stuff so easily at an early age. The difference between them and me is maybe it came too easily too soon, and then when they had to train a bit harder or work harder for success, they didn't want to because they'd been used to winning without having to put too much in. I had this determined streak and kept working, kept working. If it wasn't right, I'd go away and think about it and work a bit harder, do something else, try and change my technique or do more training. Once I've set that as my goal, I'm not going to give up on it. I'm not going to get halfway through and think it's too tough and just jack it in.'

That sense of determination, coupled with competitiveness, has given Chris the mental edge even in the toughest of circumstances. 'It's easy to be successful at small events, things where the consequences of success aren't so great,' he said. 'You can step up and produce a million times or whatever. But you cannot imagine yourself at certain points in your career, when it really comes down to the crunch.

'For me, the biggest challenge I ever overcame and I always draw upon now was the Athens Olympics. I was doing the 1,000-metre time trial. That was my event at that time. It's one rider at a time against the clock in reverse order based on world ranking. I was the world champion at the time, so I had to go last man after the end of I think 24 riders. The three guys before me, the last three guys, had all broken the world record right before I went up there.

'You're sitting there about five minutes to go and all of a sudden the goalposts are moved. Then the next guy's gone and they've moved again ... and again. So you're at the starting line literally a few seconds before you're about to get on the bike and again the chap before you has broken the world record. These were times where ... I think he was the first guy to ever go under 61 seconds for the 1,000 metres – just as I am getting up to start. Being able to not start thinking, 'Oh my God, I'm not even going to get a medal here. Four years of training and everything's all changed.' Not panicking.

'It was about being able to say, right, none of that is in your control; you have to focus on what you can control, and that is your performance. I was rehearsing in my head over and over the perfect race, from the moment when I started to the moment I finished. Having that strength. At that time I did a lot of work rehearsing beforehand, preparing for that potential situation to arise. It worked almost flawlessly. I was aware of the fact that these guys had broken the record, but it just didn't seem to register or didn't seem to bother me. I just focused on my race and it went absolutely 100 per cent as well as it could have gone. I broke the Olympic record, broke the world record, got the gold medal. It was like competing in a trance during the race. I crossed the line. It was almost easy.

'From then on, whenever I go out to a race, I think to myself, you can never be in that situation again. You can never be a not-Olympic champion trying to win your first gold medal, with all the expectation, thinking this could be your only chance. Having all that weight on your shoulders. So now it's something I draw upon and something that helps me mentally. The more you show your mental strength, the more it builds and the more you can call upon yourself to perform when you have to.'

DEDICATION

With very few exceptions, most Olympic champions sweat and grind their way to the top and do whatever it takes to get there. Sally Gunnell is a good example. 'Obviously I had a certain amount of natural talent, but I made the most of it through hard work, putting that work in … and then putting the mind in, as well, which I think comes out even bigger than the other two. I've seen people who have got massive amounts of talent who just waste it, can't put it together because they can't be bothered to train.'

Often they get a little – or a lot – of help along the way. Cathy Freeman's mother Cecilia, who Cathy 'loves and adores', gave her daughter the ultimate attitude adjustment when it seemed that she was taking her natural ability for granted, and wasn't being as focused as she needed to be. 'I'd established a bit of a local name for myself in the region as a runner and someone who had a great future ahead of her. From the age of five, I was kind of a little bit used to people creating my destiny for me. That includes my mother and stepfather, who were very integral to my journey. But there is one conversation I recall having with my mother. I had decided I wanted to go out with my friends, under the influence of my wayward teenage friends, and boys were on the scene. My mother said to me, "Catherine, I wish you were Anne-Marie," referring to my late sister, who had severe cerebral palsy and who eventually died in 1990. Although Anne-Marie wasn't intellectually disabled, she couldn't talk and she couldn't walk; she could maybe just crawl. In that moment, my mother's tough love made me realise how much I was taking for granted this natural ability and this wonderful opportunity I had at my fingertips.

'My late sister's story is one of struggle, one of loss, one of pain, and yet she was always the shining light of my life and always will be. In my mind, in my world, that memory of her is what keeps me going. Because she was the one, thanks to my mother, who helped me understand that living life to the best of my abilities was the only life I wanted to lead. My achievements give her name, her memory meaning. She's the one who inspires me. She is the one who helped me rise above anybody else or anything else, because in my mind it's just her and me alone and in my heart. That's really sacred to me. At the end of the day, I've always run for myself and for those I hold dearest to my heart, like my sister, along with others we've lost such as my ancestors.'

Cathy's motivation for achieving Olympic success is unlike any other athlete I know of. But Cathy is not your average athlete or your average person. There's a purity to the inspiration that drives her. We all like to believe that every athlete does his or her sport purely for the Olympic glory. So even though there's a lot of money involved, we like to believe that the money doesn't impact the incentive. But for most athletes that's just not true.

Initially every athlete had to be an amateur in order to compete in the Olympics. Then throughout the 1970s and 1980s, the International Olympic Committee had to start allowing athletes competing in the Olympics to be paid and be professionals, because athletes were saying, 'It's not worth that much to me if I'm not going to be able to make a living. I can't finish college and spend ten years living on scraps just to be in the Olympics.' There's no honour in being a 23- or 24-year-old watching your friends launch great careers and climb the corporate ladder, while you're sitting over here with nothing. So athletes are definitely motivated to some degree by the prospect of financial gain to become as good as they can be.

Of course, proving that you're the best not only brings monetary reward, it often brings celebrity. That too motivates many athletes.

Finally, actually achieving your potential and winning, or making an Olympic team or whatever your goal might be, is also a motivator.

When you realistically look at all three of these things – financial reward, being celebrated for being great, and delivering on your promise – the first two are easy when you have the potential. They just come automatically. You get the attention and then the endorsements, funding, sponsors and more. But you've got to work to reach your full potential.

That's the tough part, especially considering the here-and-now society we live in. The easier things come to you, the more you're going to expect them to continue to come to you. It was easy to get that contract and it was easy to get this attention and celebrity status. But now you've got to go out there and try and deliver on all that potential you're being paid for, and that's hard. That creates a problem. Having already achieved financial success and recognition without having done much to earn them makes it that much more difficult to take on the hard work and singular focus required to achieve your potential, upon which the other two goals are predicated.

DOING WHAT IT TAKES TO WIN

YOU NEED TO BE HUNGRY

If I could change one thing about many of today's athletes, it would be to instil in them the focus and the will to push themselves to the limits of their ability and then find a way to improve from there. That takes a strong focus, especially when you already have the sponsor contracts and acclaim that reward such performance. 'Okay, you're paid, people know who you are, you're getting some attention,' I would (and do) tell them. 'But don't sell yourself short. There is so much more. There's nothing like being successful as an Olympian – whether that means making an Olympic team, winning a medal, or becoming an Olympic champion, making history at the Olympic level and becoming an Olympic icon. Focus on that. Be hungry for that.'

I wish I could instil more hunger in these athletes for that dream. I think they all had it at one point, but too many don't keep that hunger. It starts to fade away because it becomes so hard. When you're 16 or 17 years old you don't have to work that hard because you're talented and got a scholarship. Endorsements and even celebrity can follow. And the easier those come, the harder it becomes to deal with the fact that you've got to work hard to really achieve your Olympic dream. The easier it is to be good, the more difficult it is to be great.

Compare that with what I experienced. When I was in college I showed potential, but I had no contracts. I got no attention. Nobody was looking at me going, 'Oh yes, Michael Johnson's going to be great.' People said, 'Michael Johnson has the potential to be great' but they didn't reward me with endorsements or sponsorship for that potential. I knew I had potential because I could see it. I'd shown it. But I knew I had to work harder because I kept getting injured at the end of every year. There was no lack of hunger. 'What have I got to do in order to get the opportunity? I've got to stop getting injured. Why am I getting injured? Because I'm not doing what I'm supposed to do. I didn't like doing weight training, but I knew I had to do it. I didn't like stretching either. I wasn't very flexible, so it was difficult. But I knew I had to do it in order to get the opportunity to compete on a world-class level. So I did the work and – boom! – instant, huge reward. Ranked number one in the world in the 200 and 400 metres. At first it was enough to achieve that. But I quickly realised that when I was hungry and went after something, I received a big pay-off.

In contrast, today's kids are handed their opportunities – and even rewards – before they've even worked for them. It's a backwards cycle that ultimately ends up being detrimental to the athlete. Belief that you deserve or are entitled to win is crap. That will get you nowhere. The belief must be that you can take the talent that you have, and that many other world-class athletes have as well, and support it with the hard work that is required. It must include figuring out how to work and train yourself most effectively to get the absolute best performance possible from your body.

I grew up during that era in sport where hard work was the difference maker. At the top level all of the athletes were naturally talented, but the harder workers were more successful. So I learned how to get the most from myself. I identified my strengths and weaknesses, and understood how *I* needed to train, as opposed to how everybody else trained.

There are different levels of work effort. Some athletes think they are working hard, even though they may not be working as hard as they can. Depending on the athlete's level of natural ability, a marginal work ethic is either fatal or not.

Mark Spitz's approach to training, which he developed around 1970 after the 1968 Mexico City Olympics in which he won two gold medals, actually put him at odds with his coach, George Haines. 'I had my own opinion on what I wanted to do,' Mark told me. 'I figured, "I'm a world record holder. I don't need to do shit that is for distance swimmers." If I didn't want to come to work out, I didn't. I viewed working out like making a deposit in a bank. If I had nothing to deposit, why would I waste my time getting more irritated? I didn't want to deposit ten cents. I'd wait until tomorrow and deposit $2.50.

'There were times I went to my two daily workouts when I thought that but I went anyway. Afterwards I'd go, "Jeeze, I didn't do jack shit, I loafed." That made me even more irritated. As a matter of fact I got so pissed off, I made an excuse to be sick the next day even though I wasn't, so I deliberately didn't have to go to training.'

Mark Spitz would probably argue with my labelling his work ethic anything but considerable. And yes, he certainly got the job done. But I can't help wondering what he would have accomplished had he made a training deposit even on those days when he didn't feel that he had much to give.

PUSHING HARD

Usain Bolt, whose skill level is extraordinarily higher than anyone else he is competing against, can get away with not working extraordinarily hard and still be an Olympic champion. But this is rare, because Usain himself is extremely rare. For starters, he doesn't exactly seem to be taking his fastest man in the world title too seriously. The majority of sports fans will probably say that his attitude is refreshing, but the competitor in me can't help but think about how much faster he could go with greater determination and hunger for the sport. Maybe that says more about me than Usain. And to be fair, his approach has worked so far.

But Usain is notorious for his stance against hard work. When I interviewed him and talked to him about whether he may take up the 400 metres some day and become the first athlete to hold world records in all three sprints, he expressed an absolute fear of the hard work required to train for the 400 metres.

'Everybody's saying, "Usain, you should do the 400 metres,"' he told me. 'Maybe after I defend my championship titles I'll be ready for it. Right now, I'm not. Work is going to be too hard, and I don't think I am prepared to dedicate all the days to the 400 metres.'

Although Usain doesn't realise it, he's already a legend in athletics. But can he focus enough to push the boundaries even further by lowering the 100- and 200-metre records and eventually taking my 400-metre record, too? He'd be the first man to hold all three, and probably the last. A superhuman. I think he can do it. I want him to, even though it would effectively write me out of the history books in many people's view. He told me he never thought he would be this big, yet I don't think he has a clue how big he really is. But that's what we like about Usain. He's running for the fun of it. The boundaries just happen to be in front of him and he has a habit of crashing through them.

The athletes who work really hard measure their work effort against the effort they are physically capable of producing. That's what I did. What my father always said was either give something your best effort or don't do it at all. Once I started training, my position was simply that every day was an opportunity for me to get better. So with that in mind, any day I missed training or any day I didn't give 100 per cent of the effort I was capable of giving would have been a missed opportunity.

Many people want to believe that it is only because of their hard work or primarily because of their hard work that they are successful, and this goes for sport as well. Nothing bothers me more than to be at a dinner party with wealthy people or successful business owners who tell you that they are self-made and that they only succeeded because of their hard work, but don't disclose the important fact that their parents were wealthy business owners or that they come from a family which provided them not only with the best education but also the seed capital to start their business and, most importantly, the 'safety net' of support if they happened to fail at their business venture. There is no underestimating the value of that safety net – and the knowledge that it is there. It increases people's confidence, and their ability to take chances and risks that they might not otherwise take and that individuals without that safety net probably wouldn't take. The same applies to athletes who boast of their hard work and talk about how they aren't as physically talented as some of their competitors but only succeeded because of their hard work and determination. They will say they worked harder than everyone else, even though they have no way of measuring their work effort against that of their competitors, who train in another country entirely and far away.

I never focused on how hard my competitors were working, since I couldn't do anything about that and it really had nothing to do with me or my goals. Just working harder than my competitors might not be enough. Great athletes and Olympic champions don't worry about other athletes and their work habits. They work as hard as they can most days. They focus their time and energy on making sure that they are giving everything they can. Weather, emergencies and changes are not excuses for missing training. If the weather is not conducive to training outside, then you move inside. If you show up at the track and there is an event going on that you didn't expect, you go to another track. If there is no other track to train on, you train on the grass, or the treadmill, or the street, or the hallway of a building. The training session may not have the quality of the planned session, but the work still gets done. My coach used to say, you could tell a champion athlete because when something happened and the coach for some reason couldn't make it to training and couldn't get a message to his athletes that he wouldn't be there, that athlete would train anyway, even if he didn't know what the training programme was for the day.

Most champions push themselves in their pursuit of excellence. The possibility of competing in the Olympics some day prompts them to push even harder.

By the time Nadia Comaneci was 11 years old her coaches were telling her that with hard work and dedication she could make it to the Olympics. 'But that's what everybody says, no?' Nadia said to me with a laugh.

'Did you believe it?' I asked.

'I did because I was improving a lot all the time. With every competition I was getting better and better. I was competitive with myself. When I was five and a half years old, my first competition involved a bicycle with three wheels. I wanted to win and I did. I wanted to be the best. It didn't matter at what. I was the kind of kid that if I put my mind to something, I was going to go all the way, giving the best that I can.'

That's what Nadia did just nine years later and for the rest of her career. 'The only thing I could do was to be the best I can be,' she said. 'Then I tried to give as much as I could from everything that I'd learned.'

Being the best she could be meant devoting herself to every part of her training. That included her conditioning regimen, which she hated as much as I hated weight work-outs and stretching. In hindsight, she too recognises just how much that hard work paid off. 'I didn't have anything broken or torn during my career, because I was physically so well prepared by conditioning,' she told me. Not only did the rigorous conditioning keep Nadia safe from injury, it helped her performance. 'It was one of the best things I did, because it's much easier to perform the gymnastic tricks when you are physically prepared.'

Like me, Nadia didn't spend a lot of time thinking about who she would be competing against. 'There was nothing I could do against the other competitors. They were training themselves, trying to be the best.' So she focused on herself, her determination to succeed compensating for her short-comings. 'Other gymnasts had more talent than I had, because I was not the springiest one,' she told me frankly. 'I wasn't the fastest. I didn't have a huge amount of flexibility. But I was willing to do more than I was asked to do. I was the kind of kid who, when my coach was asking me to do ten repetitions, I always did 12 or 15. I always did more. So even today, when I see my coach, he said he never knew what my limit was, because I always delivered more than what he asked for.'

COMMITTING 100%

Chris Hoy didn't even have coaches when he started his biking career. 'The Olympics were always the dream, but never in a million years would I have believed it was possible for a number of reasons,' he told me. 'First of all, there wasn't the pathway. There wasn't any kind of coaching infrastructure. There was no one there to guide you that way.'

So Chris filled in the gaps himself. He pursued a degree in sports science. 'I wanted to understand more about physiology, more about the human body and how we train it, how we find ways to become a better athlete, and there was no one around to give me that information.' Everything he learned in the early days of his racing career, he researched and found out for himself. 'I went and read about sprinting. I learned about muscle power, about strength development.' Then he'd head to the gym or climb on his bike and figure out by trial and error which training methods worked. 'At that time, it was so hit and miss that you'd take two steps forward, then you'd take one step back. I tended to train too much and just do too much volume of training to ever get any real adaptation to it. I look back on my training diaries from the early days and it's hilarious. I mean, I was doing three or four times the volume of work that I'm doing now.'

Armed with a basic understanding about training fundamentals thanks to his college degree, Chris added strategy to his racing. 'At that time in the UK, people were just riding their bikes and turning up at races,' he said. 'They weren't really thinking about how to get better. It was just a matter of riding their bikes and hoping for the best.' Perhaps not surprisingly, Chris's approach quickly put him at the top of the heap. At that point, even though Chris had no thoughts about cycling full-time, since there was no funding available to support that effort, he decided to try and make a go of it.

He opted for the kilometre ride, at the time one of cycling's oldest – and easiest to understand – events. Simply put, the rider who crosses the finish line first wins. 'The kilo riders, as we were known, we used to get the mickey taken out of us because we were kind of one-dimensional,' Chris said. 'We were seen as being these workhorses. We knew 100 per cent of nothing. You didn't have any judgement of speed. You didn't have any tactics. You had no awareness. It was literally just the gun would go, and you'd just go flat out and hold it for a really nasty minute.'

Chris relied on his two team-mates and rivals Jason Queally and Craig McLean during training sessions. 'They'd watch me training on the track and then give me feedback when I'd come in. 'You looked a bit rough there,' or 'You went a bit late there,' or 'Watch your technique for this bit.' Then I'd give them feedback when they were training. So we basically shared ideas and coached ourselves.'

The close-knit training group did well, with Queally earning gold in the 2000 Sydney Olympics and the trio winning silver in the team sprint. Chris would earn his first gold medal four years later at the Athens Games. 'It was a supportive network. You pushed each other on in training and encouraged each other and gave each other feedback. Queally and McLean were my training partners, rivals, team-mates and coaches all in one.'

An unexpected setback, however, almost put a halt to Chris's cycling career. In an effort to appeal to a younger audience, the International Olympic Committee (IOC) decided to introduce BMX into the 2008 Beijing Olympics, which meant that one medal event in cycling would have to be knocked out. 'The kilometre race I was doing was kind of like the blue riband event. It wasn't an event you'd imagine would ever be taken out of the programme,' Chris told me. 'I think the cycling international governing body called the IOC's bluff and said, 'Well, okay, if you're going to make us drop an event, we're going to drop the kilo time trial – the 1,000-metre time trial.' The IOC replied, 'If that's what you're going to drop, that's what you're going to drop.' At first everyone was up in arms. There were petitions and all kinds of outcry. Then it stuck and the event went.

'It took a long time to get over that, because mentally I kept thinking, "Something is going to happen and they're going to resolve this and it will be back in." It had been in the Games since cycling had been in the Games.'

Chris was wrong. Eventually he decided to try the team sprint, since the British team he'd been part of had been world champions in 2002 and 2005, and had a chance at medalling. Competition for a spot in the team, however, would be fierce. 'I had to try to strengthen my position in the team, so I thought, "I'll start riding in the two individual sprint events and that will help give me more strength and more chance of being selected for the team sprint. And in the process it will help me improve my speed." So I just started taking up these two new events and didn't think anything more about it.'

The events couldn't have been more different from what he was used to. In the sprint, suddenly strategy was as important as power and speed. 'Tactically, you can win a race or place top three in a race without necessarily being the best rider,' he explained to me. 'You could race well, you could shelter, you could position yourself well and you could improve through that. I never thought I'd be able to pick it up.'

Luckily, coaches had been brought into the sport by that point, and they were able to help shatter the mystique of the event. 'They made what had seemed like a difficult, insurmountable mountain really simple,' said Chris. 'Still, I didn't believe I could make it individually. I thought I'd just use it as a way to improve my speed and improve my chance of getting into the team sprint. "If I can do well in a sprint, then there's more chance to do more than one event," I figured. "If I've only got the team sprint and I'm very close to another athlete in terms of performance in the team sprint, if one of us had two events to do, they might take that athlete rather than the other one."'

Initially Chris didn't think he would ever become Olympic champion in either event. 'The breakthrough for one of the events came through a World Cup event,' he recalled. 'Instead of hugging the round, stalling and using tactics, I just went to the front of the race – it was a six-man race – and just powered down and strung the race out. Whereas there would have been a lot of waiting and watching each other and lots of tactics, I just went in the front and put the hammer down and won the race in the front, which was

quite an unusual thing at the time. That became my strategy, my technique, my tactic for that event. At that race a
little light bulb went off in my head. I thought, "Wow, I
think I can do this event."'

Chris would go on to become the most successful
Olympic male cyclist of all time. He did it by putting his
sport first in his life, a choice he doesn't consider a sacrifice.
'When you commit yourself 100 per cent, then everything
else becomes secondary, really,' he told me. 'From an early
age, my parents instilled this philosophy that it doesn't
matter what you do. You could be a brain surgeon or a
street cleaner. If the job's worth doing, it's worth doing
properly and to the best of your ability. The commitment
and determination to be the best that I can be – that's what's
driven me on.'

GETTING IT DONE

Athleticism coupled with this kind of hard work is an absolute requirement. As an Olympian you are competing
against the absolute best in the world and other athletes
who have superior ability just like you. So ability alone is
rarely if ever enough. But even hard work isn't enough.
You need the drive that will compel you to make the sacrifices, even if you don't call them that, necessary to be
successful.

When I asked Daley Thompson about sacrifice, he said,
'I never felt like I sacrificed. It was just automatic. I wanted
to train and work on being the best I could be. I never felt

like anything that I didn't do when I was training and preparing for competitions was a sacrifice.'

Like Chris and Daley, most Olympic champions are so driven that they don't believe they have really sacrificed much. They were both so focused on winning and being the best they could be, that was all that mattered. I have always felt this way. Now that I am retired and I compare my current lifestyle with my lifestyle when I was competing, I do see that I made some sacrifices. My eating habits are about the same, but that's because I am now making the sacrifice for my health and longevity. Besides, I've been doing that for so long it has become a way of life, so I eat pretty healthy but balanced. I have a weakness for cakes and cookies, and I like fried foods and fatty foods. I ate these foods when I was competing and I do now, but in moderation and in balance with healthy foods that I might not enjoy as much. I enjoy wine, vodka and really good Scotch. I have a glass of wine just about every day with dinner, but when I was competing I limited my alcohol beverages to weekends. At the time it didn't seem like a sacrifice, because my goal was so important to me, and I was so driven to succeed and accomplish my goal that the idea of violating my policy and drinking alcohol during the week was not an option. The same policy applied for going out and hanging out with friends. That was only a weekend activity when I was competing. I missed many friends' weddings, birthday parties and events that I would like to have attended but didn't because of my training or competition schedule. But when you're an Olympic champion your sense of commitment will actually blind you to any option other than what it takes you to refine your talent and accomplish your goal. Your path, which you are driven to follow, becomes the norm.

I don't think that anyone is perfect. I certainly know I wasn't perfect. But I was always looking to be perfect or at least as close to perfect as I could be in all ways. I can't say that this is absolutely necessary to be a great athlete, but it definitely helps. That compulsion to always improve myself is part of my personality. These days I want to be the best person I can be. Then I wanted to be the best athlete I could be. I wanted to be the best starter I could be. I wanted to be the best finisher I could be.

That perfectionism extended beyond competition day. I wanted my practices to be perfect and without mistakes or distractions. And it wasn't just my efforts at practice that I wanted to be perfect. I wanted my practice environment to be perfect and I wanted my coach to coach me perfectly. I wanted my training partners to want a perfect practice and to approach practice with all of the seriousness that was required for the practice to be perfect. Because I believe that perfection in practice will lead to perfection in the race.

Sebastian Coe, who would become a Member of Parliament for the Conservative Party and then chairman of the London Organising Committee for the Olympic Games after heading up London's successful bid to host the 2012 Summer Olympics, felt the same way. 'When you and I were training, you and I craved criticism,' he said during our interview. 'You're always wanting to absorb information and support and help that might make you that much quicker or that much higher.'

That quest for perfection is something that any athlete who is going to be great must possess, especially at the Olympic level. Growing up, however, that wasn't my strong suit. My dad, who was a perfectionist and expected the same from me, changed that. When I was a teenager, to make extra money I mowed the lawns of some of the neighbours in the community. One day I was home doing my homework when my dad came home and walked into my room. 'Did you mow Mrs Williams's yard today?' he asked.

'Yes, I did,' I answered. As usual, she had told me what good work I had done before paying me.

'I drove by there on my way home and you did a pitiful job,' he said bluntly. 'As soon as you finish your homework, you go back down there and do it right.'

My dad was always on to me to be the best I could be and didn't accept less, no matter what it was. And in so doing he taught me to do the same. Many athletes, however, don't have that perfectionism personality trait.

I sought perfection in every race. To achieve that, I also had to demand perfection from myself in every practice, which is why those were always closed to onlookers. My track workouts were dictated not only by my coach, but by the beeper which I encountered on my first day of training at the Baylor Track in 1986, and which I described in detail in Chapter 1. I always wanted to be on or ahead of the beeper. That was the only way to make sure that a 26-second

200-metre interval was really a 26-second 200-metre interval.

I recognised early on that it was easier to run really fast at the beginning of an interval run, and be far ahead of the beeper, which meant I could coast at the end of the run when I was fatigued and be back on the beeper by the end of the run. But that didn't provide effective training. So my objective was to be on the beeper at all times. If I got ahead of the beeper at any point during the interval run, then I demanded that I finish the run that far ahead or more.

THE DIFFERENCE IS IN THE DETAILS

For me attention to detail was – and continues to be – everything. This is where focusing on the small things comes into play. You can't be perfect by just making sure that the big things are all okay. You have to make sure the small details have been taken care of as well. That included making sure practice tracks would be available when we were on the road, making sure we started practice on time, making sure the beeper was set on the right time by timing it against my watch in order to ensure that I was running the time that the workout called for. I'd also check the weather at the beginning of each week to know what training gear to take with me when travelling to train with Coach, since I needed to focus on training without the distraction of being too cold or wet.

That kind of planning down to the smallest detail came easily to me. My father was a planner. When you're in control and have a plan, you're less likely to be surprised. As someone who is easily embarrassed, having a plan for every eventuality meant that I would be less likely to be surprised. Fewer surprises meant less embarrassment. Naturally, I wanted to be just like him. So I learned to plan and manage the details that derail others.

Some people, however, have personality traits that make them less effective when it comes to sweating the details.

FOR BETTER OR WORSE

Recognising one's weaknesses – whether mental or physical – and doing what it takes to improve is an essential component of Olympic success. Take Mark Spitz.

'What do you think your greatest accomplishments were, Mark?' a reporter asked him at a press conference in Sydney, Australia.

'Obviously winning seven gold medals,' Mark answered.

'No, I don't think that's it,' said the Australian reporter, who knew swimming as well as a British sports reporter would know football.

'Okay, I'm game,' Mark said. 'Tell me what my greatest accomplishment was.'

'When I analyse all of the years you've been swimming, and not counting prelims or semi-finals, on the day you basically swam in national championships, international meets, Pan-Am games [there were no World Championships when Mark competed] and the Olympic Games, you swam 76 times, and you had 35 world records. Basically, 50 per cent of the time you swam, you broke a world record. But more importantly, the last 20 times you were in the water you broke 19 world records, and you won all 20 of those races. That is your greatest accomplishment.'

Mark must have had an occasional bad day during those competitions. But he still managed to win. 'I just figured that winning was a matter of making one or two less mistakes,' Mark told me. 'I think that's pretty common with a lot of great athletes, that they knew what their weaknesses were. I always concentrated on trying to improve those.

'There's a film of me when I finished my very last individual event in the Olympic games. I only had one event left to win the seventh gold medal the next day in the relay. You see my coach putting his hand around me, pointing his finger at me and giving me instruction. You can read my lips as I reply, "I know what you're saying." Even at that point he was still instructing me on all the mistakes I made even through my last event, because it was always a work in progress.'

Athletes not only have to constantly learn about themselves, they have to want to perfect themselves as people and as athletes. Even though perfection is almost impossible to achieve, you always have to strive to get as close as possible to that goal. Only through that quest will you continue to address those areas that still need improving. Over the years there have been debates in sport about whether you should train to your strengths or train to your weaknesses. Most people, myself included, believe you must train to both. But when it comes down to where the balance lies, even though there is no one uniform strategy for success, I think that the best athletes focus more on their flaws.

Of course, some weaknesses can't be fixed. So you must also accept those inherent shortcomings that you can't change and make adjustments accordingly. Happily, just the awareness of your deficiencies can be a huge help, because that awareness allows you to compensate by building in special features to your routine or programme.

Early in my career my training group always did strength training after our track training sessions. At that point I was already fatigued from the track session, so not only was I not mentally motivated for the strength session, which I never cared for, I was not physically motivated either. So while I would never skip a session, I could tell sometimes when I completed that session that I had not given 100 per cent.

I knew that this was something about me that wasn't going to change, no matter how much I wanted it to change, and so I made an adjustment in my programme and started doing my strength training sessions in the mornings. I would wake up, eat breakfast, give myself an hour and a half to get going and meet my strength coach for my weight training session. I also hired a strength coach who I knew would never allow me to slack in those sessions, because as much as I wanted to have 100 per cent effective strength training sessions, knowing how important they were to my career, I also knew I could not depend on myself and my willpower alone.

I use that same strategy now as I try to maintain my fitness in a post-competitive life. Because I've trained for the better part of my life to be athletically fit, people tend to think that even now that I am no longer competing I must be this workout fanatic who has to train every day just to be happy and make it through life – but for me that couldn't be further from the truth. It is very difficult for me to go out and put my body through physical stress for an obvious reward in terms of health, but one that will never compare with the reward of winning races. For years after I first retired I tried to go out in the afternoon for training and found that, just like when I tried to do strength training in the afternoon, I was unsuccessful. Since this was not a job or a career, instead of going out in the afternoon for training and giving a less than 100 per cent effort, many times I would just delay until it was evening and too late to train. So I started getting up in the morning and getting my training done first thing. It still takes a bit of tough self-talk and some serious willpower to do it, but now I get them done.

Successful athletes know themselves very well. Most of the time this comes from the ability to step outside oneself and do a serious objective analysis of themselves. This approach, which is an incredibly valuable tool when it comes to identifying and self-correcting flaws and weaknesses, is at every athlete's disposal. It came naturally to me, but in working with other athletes I have come to realise that it doesn't always come naturally. Some athletes find it easier to make excuses for their flaws or just to ignore them altogether. Or sometimes they feel they can afford to let those flaws or weaknesses exist because superior talent and hard work will help them succeed. But if you want to be the absolute best you can be, you must always seek out and correct any flaw or weakness.

When Steve Redgrave acknowledged his weaknesses, it made all the difference in his performance. 'I've always been more of an explosive athlete, and rowing is more endurance,' he told me. 'It's good to have the speed and the power, but my downfall in international rowing at the beginning of my career was that I could blast off the start and get a lead on almost anybody, and then sort of struggle, and then in the closing stages of the race I could come flying back at people. But I could never maintain it all the way through.

'Because rowing is a muscular endurance sport – so it's good to be big and strong – it's about how much training you do. So you can technically be very bad, but if you train really hard you can get really good results. There's a saying in rowing that if you can't catch, throw or kick a ball, your sport is rowing. For a very co-ordinated sport, we have a whole host of people that are not that well co-ordinated that end up winning Olympic gold medals, because of the repetitiveness of the sport – just going in and grinding away. You can improve from that point of view.'

Steve, however, recognised that he needed to do more than put in the miles. So he and his coach at the time, Mike Spracklen, an extremely good technical coach, began to look at training regimens in other sports to figure out how best to work on Steve's endurance limitations. One of those sports was swimming.

'Swimmers tend to plough up and down, apart from the 50-metre guys, and work on endurance all the time,' says

Steve. 'So that's what we started to do. I had this natural power and speed but couldn't maintain it. So I started doing more miles, making the speed last longer.

'Mike had this theory that time in the boat is well spent, even if you're sitting in it and not doing anything. You're sort of becoming in harmony with the boat and more sympathetic towards it. In some ways he was right, but miles make champions. The more training you do, the fitter you become, the stronger you become. Yes, your technique improves with it, because if you're out there doing a rowing session, you're not just working physically, you're going to work on your technique as well.'

Suddenly, within 12 months of being eliminated at the World Championships – not even in the top 12 – Steve was holding his own with the top guys worldwide in single sculls. Just two months before the 1984 Los Angeles Olympics he jumped into a coxless four with Matthew Pinsent, Tim Foster and James Cracknell, and the team became the favourite to win the Olympics. Steve had been good enough to win most of his races in the UK. Instead of settling for national acclaim, however, he ferreted out his weaknesses and then strove to correct them.

TRAINING SMART

That kind of smart training has proved to be the difference between Olympic athletes and Olympic champions over the last several years. The fact that an athlete works hard doesn't necessarily mean that he's getting better or getting closer to accomplishing his goal. When I first made the decision to focus equally on being the best in the world at 200 metres and at 400 metres, my coach and I had to develop one training programme that would be effective for my improvement and development in both events. We knew training twice a day would be impossible, at least if the training sessions were to have the quality of effort required. So each session had to be as effective as possible. As my coach and I developed my training programme, I made sure that each training session was effective at helping me to improve. I wanted to understand exactly what Coach had me doing each training session and exactly how doing that training session was going to help me to run a faster 200 metres or a faster 400 metres or to beat my competitors.

Since I retired and started Michael Johnson Performance, my training staff and I have been obsessed with the effectiveness of our training programmes. So we have taken the concept of 'smart training' to a whole other level from when I was competing. We liken our philosophy to a rifle approach, as opposed to a shotgun approach. With a shotgun you get a lot of small attempts at hitting the target. With the rifle you have to put more time into aiming, but you have a much bigger and more effective bullet to hit the target. We have found that when we take this approach in designing all of our training programmes, and most importantly when we educate our athletes while training them, they improve more rapidly.

The more the athlete knows about the training programme and how it will help him to improve, the better he will execute the training sessions and thus the more effective the training will be in helping him reach his goal. Nowadays the Olympic champion athlete understands this and takes an active role in developing his training programme. The work doesn't stop with just physically showing up every day to train and give maximum physical effort. The athlete must also engage intellectually and work in partnership with coaches and trainers to develop the most effective training programme to help him to be the best he can be both physically and mentally.

5.

MENTAL GAMES

People often ask me how much of success in sport is physical and how much is mental. I always answer that it doesn't matter. What's most important is the acknowledgement and acceptance that there is a mental component to sporting success. Once you know that, then there should be an automatic desire to become as good and as skilled as you can possibly be at the mental part of your sport. Olympic champion athletes strive to be as good as they can be mentally and don't concern themselves with whether 80 per cent or 20 per cent of their sport is mental. They want to be 100 per cent proficient at the mental part of their sport, just as they want to be 100 per cent proficient physically.

You have to be careful with the idea of positive thinking, because all the positive thinking in the world won't help you to be successful and achieve your goals if you're not prepared and if you haven't put in the work. One of the very few things I was aware of that could make me feel fearful, not too confident and unable to think positively prior to a race was if I had not prepared properly in the days, weeks and months leading up to it. Preparation is everything. And I dealt with that every day. I didn't want to feel when I stepped on the line that I wasn't ready. I wanted to feel, 'I know I'm ready because I have done everything possible to be ready.' That motivated me to go out and work as hard as I possibly could and leave nothing on the track. I gave absolutely 100 per cent every single day, so that when the time came and I was in that call room – my favourite time – with the seven other athletes who would be lining up against me, I could feel as confident as I could possibly be and probably more confident than anyone else in that room. I knew I had the talent, I knew I had prepared, I knew I had worked as hard as I could possibly work. Having done everything I possibly could, I could just go out and run and let the chips fall where they may.

I learned during my Olympic career that in sport, as in anything else, it is not enough just to train hard. Training is important without a doubt, and so is execution. What often gets ignored is preparation. Preparation is required in order to take the benefit of the training and apply it to the execution. In those few days when the hard training period was over and I was waiting for race day, I always spent the time focused on preparation for the race. I'd think of all the scenarios before the race, just prior to the race and during the race, and have a plan for each scenario and for perfecting that plan. I also spent that time assessing all of the things

TOP LEFT: My Nike gold shoes, custom made for me for the 1996 Olympic Games in Atlanta. A bold start to my quest to make history. *(AFP/Getty Images)*

TOP RIGHT: Running the curve ahead of Great Britain's Roger Black in the 400m final. *(Sports Illustrated/Getty Images)*

BOTTOM: On the podium, having won my first individual Olympic gold medal. Despite trying to be in control and private through most of my career, I finally allowed myself to let go and feel the joy … and that's when I started to cry. *(AFP/Getty Images)*

TOP LEFT: Me with my brother and sisters in the back garden of our house in 1972 (I was four years old here). From left to right: Paul Jr., me, Regina, Deidre and Cheryl. As I was the youngest my sisters and brother would always chase me around and tease me. I *had* to get fast!

TOP RIGHT: With my son Sebastian in 2004. I do mandate that he participate in some sport, but equally I mandate that he participate in music and art.

MIDDLE: With my mother Ruby and father Paul. Parents play a major role in the success of many Olympic champions, and I'm certainly no different.

BOTTOM: The day I signed my scholarship papers to compete for Baylor University. Left to right: Clyde Hart (my coach), his wife Maxine, my mother, me, my father and Que McMaster (assistant coach at Baylor).

TOP: Usain Bolt blew my mind when he smashed the 100m world record in the final at the 2008 Games in Beijing. *(Getty Images)*

BOTTOM LEFT: Rebecca Adlington with her gold medal for the 800m freestyle in Beijing. She broke the 19-year-old world record in the final and became the most successful British swimmer in more than 100 years. *(AFP/Getty Images)*

BOTTOM RIGHT: Chris Hoy celebrates winning gold in the track cycling sprint, an event he took on after his preferred race was taken out of the Olympic programme. He took three gold medals home from Beijing. *(Getty Images)*

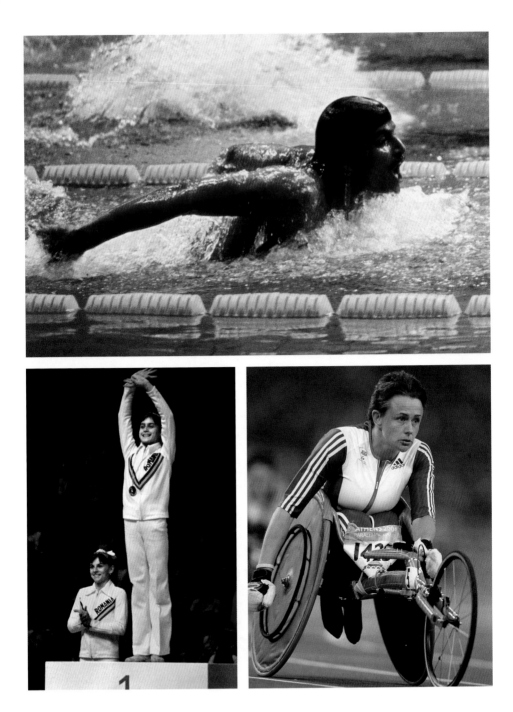

TOP: Mark Spitz in action at the 1972 Munich Olympics, where he won an incredible seven gold medals. *(AFP/Getty Images)*

BOTTOM LEFT: Nadia Comaneci celebrates gold in the uneven bars at the 1976 Montreal Olympics at the age of just 14, after she became the first person in Olympic history to score a perfect 10. *(AFP/Getty Images)*

BOTTOM RIGHT: Paralympian Tanni Grey-Thompson, who won a mind-boggling 16 Olympic medals, including 11 golds. *(Getty Images)*

TOP LEFT: Jackie Joyner-Kersee takes off on her way to gold in the long jump at the 1988 Seoul Olympics. Jackie was an athlete I grew up watching and continued to look up to throughout my career. *(Getty Images)*

TOP RIGHT: Ian Thorpe, who broke his ankle just ten months before the Sydney Olympics in 2000, celebrates gold in the 400m freestyle. Ian's experience could serve as a lesson for any injured athlete. *(Getty Images)*

BOTTOM: 'I remember crossing the finish line and thinking, "Am I in a dream or has that really happened?"' Sally Gunnell celebrates gold in the 400m hurdles at the Barcelona Olympics in 1992. *(Getty Images)*

TOP LEFT: Daley Thompson preparing to throw in the shot putt on his way to gold in the decathlon at the 1984 Los Angeles Olympics. *(Getty Images)*

TOP RIGHT: 'I was so overcome that I didn't know what to do but sit down and take my shoes off.' Cathy Freeman after winning the 400m at the Sydney Olympics in 2000. *(Getty Images)*

BOTTOM LEFT: Steve Redgrave with his gold medal at the Sydney Olympics. He won a gold at five consecutive Olympics, spanning a period of 16 years. *(Getty Images)*

BOTTOM RIGHT: Seb Coe winning gold in the 1500m final in Los Angeles 1984. 'Winning is predicated on a pretty healthy, robust diet of defeat,' says the two-time Olympic champion. *(Getty Images)*

TOP LEFT: Me and Coach (Clyde Hart) at the Baylor University football stadium in Waco, Texas, in 1992 – just before we headed to Barcelona for the Olympics.

TOP MIDDLE: On the winner's podium with my 400m gold medal at the Sydney Olympics in 2000.

TOP RIGHT: Record-breaking footwear – the purple shoes in my hands I wore to break the 200m world record in the US Olympics trials in 1996, and the gold shoes in Coach's hands I wore to break *that* record in the Olympic final.

BOTTOM: Some of the Laureus Sport for Good Foundation members – including some of the stars of this book. Left to right: (front row) Daley Thompson, me, Nadia Comaneci, Nawal El Moutawakel, Emerson Fittipaldi, Edwin Moses, Franz Klammer, Sean Fitzpatrick; (back row) Kip Keino, Mark Spitz, Hugo Porta, Ilie Nastase, Robby Naish, Boris Becker, Kapil Dev, Morne du Plessis.

TOP: *Yes!* Winning double Olympic gold – with a new world record. I've never felt anything like it in my life. *(AFP/Getty Images)*

BOTTOM: With my 200m gold medal, alongside my friend and great rival Frankie Fredericks (who took silver, on the right) and bronze medallist Ato Boldon. *(Getty Images)*

I might have to deal with and any potential distractions, and making a plan to control the potential distractions and things I might need to deal with and understanding and preparing to be ready for any that I might not be able to control.

Before the 2000 Olympics in Sydney, I was invited to Australia for an appearance about nine months prior to the Games. It was something that ordinarily I would have probably declined, but I saw it as an opportunity to get to Sydney to scout out the situation, including the distance from the city to the stadium, which actually lay outside the city centre, and also to get an understanding of the best place for me to stay and train. This was all about knowing what my situation would be, what to expect and how to control as much of my environment as possible.

During the Olympic competition, I opted, for the third time in my career, not to stay in the athletes' village. But that meant I would be quite far from the stadium and would need to work through those logistics. Ultimately, after considering everything including a helicopter shuttle service back and forth each day, my team and I had a plan in place that I'd approved and felt 100 per cent comfortable with. I had a three-bedroom suite in a hotel in the city centre, with restaurants within walking distance and room service, another hotel ten minutes from the stadium, and two dedicated drivers with vans to transport me and my team. The French Olympic team had a training centre about 30 minutes from my hotel to which they had exclusive access with no media or unauthorised persons allowed. I worked out a deal with them for access to their training complex. My plan was to stay in the hotel in the city centre and train at the French complex each day until the day before my first race, and then move into my other hotel close to the stadium. At that point my wife and my son, who was only three months old at the time, would move into the hotel suite in the city centre. Everything was planned from a logistical standpoint months in advance. That allowed me in the days before my race to focus just as diligently on preparing my mind.

Since the end of my career I have continued to devote a significant amount of time and energy to preparation when it comes to accomplishing any goal, because of how well that worked for me as an athlete. Nowadays, as the owner of a sports performance training company that hosts several events each year with professional sporting teams like Arsenal FC and the Dallas Cowboys, along with individual athletes, I am constantly stressing to my staff the importance of understanding every potential problem. In pursuit of my goals of winning and maintaining business, we need to have a plan to address any issue that could come up, and eliminate potential problems or obstacles to a successful event before they occur. My staff have found that this not only minimises the chances of anything negatively affecting our event, it also increases the effectiveness of our operation and execution of the event. Because of the planning, as an organisation we go into the occasion with much more confidence, much less worry, and the ability to focus on running an excellent event. In short, we know we've prepared on all fronts. We're ready, as ready as I used to be in the blocks before every race I ran.

Like me, Sally Gunnell, who calls herself a 'confidence runner', had to go into a race knowing that she'd 'done every training session, eaten well, and just really focused so that when I could stand on the line I'd ticked every box'. Sally, however, found even more ways to give herself confidence. 'We got into this pre-championship routine of always going to a Chinese restaurant and having a fortune cookie. Luckily they were always brilliant. I remember the one before Barcelona was "You are the chosen one." My husband John would always give me little lucky charms. I did have a little bag of lucky stones, which I lost about six months before I retired. And I had the routine of getting ready.'

FINDING THAT WINNING EDGE

For a bunch of people who have worked as hard – or harder – than most to excel at what we do, we athletes are an amazingly superstitious bunch. Nadia Comaneci admitted to me that each time she walked into an arena she would lead with the same foot. 'Every time there was a door, it had to be the right foot. But if something happened in a competition and it didn't go well, then I was changing and would go with the left foot!'

Superstitions notwithstanding, one of the keys to Olympic success is establishing a formula for success that the athlete can revisit again and again in the good times and the bad times. This establishes consistency and longevity over the span of his or her career. My training sessions were the key for me and quickly led me to a remarkable string of victories.

Even though my confidence started to soar when I began to do so much better in my races than my opponents were doing in theirs, I made sure not to get complacent. At the end of the year I'd take all the trophies I'd won at championships and invitational races around the world that year and box them up. Stripping all my trophies off the living-room shelf reminded me that the season was finished and everything would start over fresh the next year. At the start of the following season I would once more feel the drive to fill that shelf up with trophies again.

I knew there was a danger of feeling I was invincible. You want to feel like that during the race, but you don't ever want to start to believe that. This can be a very difficult challenge for athletes. You often hear that it's easier to stay on top than to get to the top. They're both difficult, but there is an assumption that once you've made the climb it's easier to maintain that lofty height. While that may be true, you should never underestimate the difficulty of sustaining a level of success. And keep in mind that when you're on top there's a lot more to lose and a longer way to fall.

After my success in 1996 in Atlanta, I found myself in this situation in a major way. I had not only dominated for six years at that point, I had established myself as the undisputed superstar of the sport. The way I had been successful prior to 1996, however, would no longer be the right formula, and I realised that. To try to use the same type of motivation and tactics to get the best performance from myself and to win races, including the major championships and even the next Olympics, would be a mistake. I was a different athlete now and was perceived differently now as well. What I had accomplished changed everything.

So I had to balance the formula for success that had gotten me to that point with a new way of approaching competition, setting goals and achieving success that would be effective for me over the next four years. Up to that point in my career my primary focus had been on competing. I liked the feeling of finishing first. I seriously went into every race wanting not only to win but to cross the finish line as far ahead of the field as possible. After each race the primary two statistics I immediately focused on were how fast I had run the race and how big the gap was between me and second place. I was keenly aware of who among my competitors was starting to get some hope based on a closer than normal race with me. My goal would be to race him again and crush that hope by beating him to a point of feeling embarrassed that he ever even thought he might get me!

I had also, of course, been motivated by the desire to become an Olympic champion. I had not only accomplished that, I had made Olympic history. I realised those could no longer be my motivation and that I had to find new motivation. In addition, I would have to contend with the fact that now losing a race would be bigger news than winning a race.

It took a little bit of time for me to realise all of these things and make the necessary adjustments, but ultimately

I did. I had always enjoyed making history in the sport and doing things that hadn't been done before, so I started to focus less on just winning the races and more on what mark I would leave on the sport after my retirement. And my main motivation was breaking the 400-metre world record before I left the sport. That shift enabled me to continue to dominate for another four years and win in Sydney.

I have applied that same lesson to my life after sport. I understand now that my goals and motivation and how I achieve success are fluid and require constant adjustments. I only make those necessary adjustments after carefully considering all the factors. They're based on striking the right balance between, on the one hand, the formula or structure responsible for success in the past, and, on the other, what might be different in the road ahead and what might be needed for the road ahead. When Michael Johnson Performance started up as a company with only four employees, we were trying to establish ourselves and win customers' trust. Four years later we are in a growth stage, having established a brand that is known for quality training programmes and services, along with innovative ways of getting the best results from athletes. Not only do we have different goals now, but we also have more to protect. So how we operate has had to change to some degree.

Whether as an athlete or a business owner, these are hard choices to make, and the wrong one can be as fatal to a business as it is to an Olympic career. But these choices and decisions are critical components of success. And with the right nurturing, that success can feed upon itself.

MENTAL GAMES

As an athlete, it's easier when you win. The race isn't as much of a struggle. Part of the reason for that is you feel more in control during the race if you're winning. If someone's in front of me and I am not winning, then they're dictating the race and I am reacting to them. I'm trying to catch them, outrun them and do something in reaction to what they're doing. By contrast, when I am winning the race I am in charge. The race requires less effort because I'm not making adjustments, I'm not trying as hard. It's just coming easy.

A SPANNER IN THE WORKS

Even with all the talent and training in place, however, there are no guarantees. I remember talking with my training partners about a month before the 1992 Olympic trials. We had all qualified and would be competing to be on the team. They were all going to be contesting the 400 metres and I had decided to contest the 200 metres. When I made a point about the competitors in the 200 metres, one of them remarked that there was no point in putting odds on that event because I was going to win it. It was sort of a strange moment for me. After training to make the Olympic team all this time, it became clear to me that in order for me *not* to make the team I would have to really mess up.

When I got to the Olympic trials I ran the best race I had ever run, clocking a personal best of 19.79 and only missing the world record by 0.07 seconds. A few weeks later I followed that up with another personal best, in the 400 metres, running 43.98 seconds. I was in the best shape of my career. And then I came down with food poisoning just two weeks before the Olympics, and it wrecked my body. I didn't even make it to the final. I sat in Barcelona watching guys who had never beaten me before take medals that could have been mine. It was the biggest disappointment of my life and my career.

Anything can – and does – happen at the Olympics. It's how you deal with the challenges and setbacks that makes the difference. Sebastian Coe's story illustrates how elite athletes have to be able to roll with the punches.

'Winning is predicated on a pretty healthy, robust diet of defeat,' he told me when I interviewed him. 'You've got to learn to deal with that, and smart people know how to build out of it and what they need to do to address those issues.' That's precisely what he was forced to do during the 1980 Olympics when, despite being in the best physical condition of his life, nervousness, inexperience and colder than usual temperatures got the better of him. 'I just had a bad day in the office,' he says. 'I broke five cardinal rules in 800-metre running. One of them would have been terminal, so five of them, there just was no way.'

When you have Seb's level of talent, a bad day doesn't mean tanking completely. But it does mean missing out on a gold medal that you had been expected to win and having to settle for silver. The day after the race, Seb was so distraught that he didn't even want to get out of bed. Then into his room marched British decathlete Daley Thompson, as Seb recalls. 'I said something really lame like, "What's the weather like out there?" He ripped the curtains open and went, "It all looks a bit silver to me."'

Daley remembers the story differently. 'I actually said, "It looks cloudy with a chance of silver."'

Seb Coe can now laugh about Daley's unique brand of psychotherapy, but at the time he had to regroup in a hurry for his next event. 'I ran for an hour to clear my head and came to terms with two things. One, statistically the chances of running that badly again were on my side. You can't possibly do that in the next couple of years. Second, I got to the point where I genuinely did not care whether I won, I lost or I was second, third, fourth or fifth. It was clear in my mind that I would never again walk off a track knowing that I had so underperformed. You don't become a bad athlete overnight. One races sometimes against the odds, and falls back on numbers.'

Seb also talked about the importance of being a student of one's event, including learning how those who came before you won or lost. 'I'd pretty much read most of the good athletics biographies and autobiographies by the time I was 20. I'd read the Jim Ryun story. I remember very vividly that in 1972, when Jim got seeded in the wrong race because they looked at his mile time and not his 1500 metre time, he ended up in a field that was inexperienced. Effectively Jim's career ended that day in the Olympic Games. I was extraordinarily lucky that I had the opportunity to get back on a track within three days and address that.'

MENTAL STRENGTH AND STUDY

Success at the highest level requires this brand of mental fortitude. Ironically, Daley, who was such a loose cannon compared with Seb – who has always been a diplomatic, British darling – shared that strength of spirit along with the determination to better himself by studying his sport. Daley's learning curve started even before his career had officially been launched. 'I've always been a student of whatever I'm doing. I want to learn so much that I will read and learn everything I possibly can about whatever it is that I'm doing,' he told me. 'So when there was an English schools championship coming up in a couple of weeks, I went to the library and picked up a book about how to run faster. It said to do three lots of 300-metre runs in one session twice a week and two lots of 500-metre runs in a session twice a week, so that's what I did.'

Later, after he had begun to experience success as a decathlete, he got to know Bruce Jenner. Every time he saw him, he tried to pick Jenner's brain about the decathlon. Eventually, Daley asked so many questions that he drove Jenner crazy. 'I don't like talking to you,' Jenner snapped. 'I don't want to talk to you any more.'

As Seb and Daley understood full well, understanding the ins and outs of their sport provided them with an edge that non-students couldn't compete with. Both also understood the power of their minds to make or break an athletic career.

While positive thinking and self-belief aren't remotely enough in and of themselves, without them success is impossible. Daley has always assumed he could do anything. Like me and other Olympic athletes including Rebecca Adlington, he focused on the upcoming race rather than his competitors. 'I felt I was going to win,' he told me. When I asked him where that confidence came from, he said simply, 'It's all I've ever known.'

Daley grew up knowing he would be successful. 'From the time I was a kid, I always believed I was going to do something special,' he told me. 'My brothers and sisters were just normal hard-working people and so was my mother, but I believed I could be great at something.' Like me, he didn't think early on that his success would involve sport, especially considering the lack of support from his family on that front. Eventually, however, his athletic talent was too great to deny. 'At one point I thought I could be the best footballer in the world,' he said. 'Then I thought I could be the best track athlete in the world.'

The latter proved true. Indeed, considering the ten events it takes to become decathlon champion, it could be argued that Daley became the world's greatest athlete, period.

Success like Daley's requires talent, hard work and, yes, belief. The belief that you have the talent, ability, desire, work ethic, and everything else required to achieve your dream sustains you in the face of inevitable setbacks and obstacles. I'm not talking about unjustified belief that you can achieve your goal, but real, justified belief backed up by supporting facts.

Olympic champions don't just believe in themselves because of what they want. They believe in themselves because they know they've got what it takes. People often ask me when I knew I was fast. 'When I started running fast,' I answer. As for when I knew that I would become an Olympic champion, my answer is I knew I *could* become an Olympic champion when I proved to myself that I could run as fast as the athletes winning the medals.

Usain Bolt always believed in himself because he had proved to himself just how fast he really was. At the 2004 Olympics, when sports writers from all over the world were asking whether Usain was going to succeed and why he wasn't doing better if he was such a talent, he said to the Jamaican team's press attaché, 'Listen to them talk. What will they say in two years' time?' He knew he would be great.

That doesn't mean that those athletes who go on to become Olympic legends don't have doubts. Champions question themselves more than outsiders do. They have a healthy dose of scepticism, but understand that their doubts could help push them to high achievement. In fact, I think that really big dose of scepticism that my father taught me to have has helped me more than anything else.

Of course, questioning oneself only helps if the rest of the mental building blocks are in place on the day of competition. Mental preparation is not just about the mental toughness required to deal with the pressure to perform and deliver in the heat of the battle. It's also knowing and understanding yourself as an athlete, knowing and understanding your sport and your event, and knowing and understanding the best way for you to compete so as to deliver your best performance consistently. This is not easy to accomplish, especially since there is no textbook or manual to tell you exactly how it's done. At the Olympic level, where everyone is supremely talented, it's all about the small improvements that will make the big differences. Those small changes and details go beyond just working hard. The winning formula lies in the effectiveness of what you're doing.

I started learning about myself as an athlete and a person when I was a university athlete. Throughout my career I continued to learn about myself and what mindset I needed to be in, what my training environment needed to be like to have my best training, and how to control my environment at competitions in order to be best prepared for the race. Until I retired, I would search for an understanding of myself, make adjustments and set up my team to process the information I had about myself in order to be able to perform at my best.

From my days competing for Baylor University, I would watch video of myself as often as I could. The father of my team-mate and good friend Todd Thompson would come and videotape every race we competed in. I would study each tape again and again, repeatedly hitting rewind in order to assess how I was running the race from the gun to the finish line.

Today video analysis is a major tool of Michael Johnson Performance. We use a computerised software programme that allows us to break down athletics movements at 1,000 frames per second and do some amazing analysis. I didn't have that when I was competing, so I did what I had to and became a master at pressing the pause and play buttons to stop the tape at exactly the point I needed in the race in order to understand how I was running the race. I would also compare a tape of a recently run race with a previous race and contrast the two to understand why I had run faster or slower.

In addition, I was always interested in other sprinters and how they ran their races, so I videotaped professional athletes running races at televised events. I had a tape of the 1987 World Championships from Rome with Calvin Smith winning the 200 metres which I watched repeatedly for tips on how to run a fast 200 metres. On that same tape I had Butch Reynolds, who had broken the world record earlier that year for 400 metres, losing the world championship. I watched that race repeatedly as well, trying to figure out how he lost a race he probably should have won. My study of my sport didn't stop there. I would watch any track competition on television and try to gain tips about how to sprint better or even what mistakes to avoid.

After graduation from Baylor with a marketing degree and starting my professional career in 1990, I had a lot of time on my hands because I no longer had class each day. I briefly considered continuing to go to school to get a masters degree in business. That would fill my day and continue the routine, but I truly did not care much for school at that point. So I spent most of my afternoons before training watching races and even taking notes on the library of taped race footage that I had accumulated of my own races and the races of others. My training partners Tony Miller and Deon Minor, who worked with me during the first four years of my career, would come to my house to watch races with me, and we would debate late into the night about different athletes and race strategies.

I was always most critical of myself. After every race of my professional career, I immediately assessed how I had run the race and focused on any mistakes. If I didn't run as fast as I expected, I tried to figure out the reason for the poor performance. If I had a good race, I would assess that too, to understand what I did to run so well, so that I could duplicate that performance.

Early on in my career I had established a base race strategy for the 200 metres and a separate strategy for the 400. Over the years I would study those strategies and make tweaks to each of them in races to try to improve my times. Sometimes those adjustments worked and sometimes they didn't. I had to be careful because, in athletics, you're not just running against the clock to run a faster time. You're also racing against the competition to get to the finish line, since that is what the sport is all about. Too much focus on trying to run a faster time and any radical change from the strategy that had proven successful in winning races could result in a loss, so I had to be careful when deciding how to tweak a race strategy and how much risk to take.

As a result, my effort to improve my personal best over the years proved to be a very slow process. For example, in the 200 metres my first big breakthrough race was when I ran 19.90 seconds in 1990 at the US championships. I consistently ran under 20 seconds for 200 metres for the next two years and improved to 19.79 seconds in 1992 at the US Olympic trials. I felt surely at that point that I was close to being able to break the world record of 19.72 set by Pietro Mennea in 1979. It wasn't till four years later, in 1996, that I was able to shave just 13 hundredths of a second off my personal best and set a new world record of 19.66. Ultimately, I was able to take another 34 hundredths off that, running 19.32 a month later.

The reason that record-breaking performance was so special and is widely regarded as one of the most incredible performances in the history of the sport is due to how much I took off the previous record. Of course some of that improvement wasn't just due to the changes in the race strategy but also to my coach and me making adjustments in our training programme. That required an understanding by Coach and me that went beyond the established ideas and concepts for 200-metre training. For me to achieve the best performance I was capable of producing in that race, we had to couple our understanding of me as an athlete with our understanding of the event and develop a totally customised training programme and race strategy.

The 400 metres is not only twice the distance of my other event, but the process of developing a customised training programme and race strategy for it is at least twice as difficult. Because the race is twice as long and because your body suffers from fatigue at the end of this race, there is a much bigger margin for error. In fact, even though I came first in all but two of my 400-metre races during my 11-year career, I rarely walked off the track without imme-diately identifying at least one mistake in the race I'd just won. Because it is such a long sprint, no one, not even the best in the world, can run full speed for the entire 400 metres. That makes it a very difficult race to run. As a result, a big part of the race strategy has to be managing energy, because there isn't enough to last the full race if you go all out.

My breakthrough race in the 400 metres also came in 1990, when I ran 44.29 seconds. Later that year I improved to 44.27 and then 44.21. Two years later, in 1992, I dipped under 44 seconds, running 43.98. Over the next seven years I would consistently run under 44 seconds, and I finished my career with more sub-44-second times than anyone in the history of the event. In 1995 I won the 400 metres world championship, just missing the world record by one tenth of a second when the clock stopped at 43.39. After breaking the world record in the 200 the next year, I focused my attention on breaking the 400-metre world record before retirement. Even though I concentrated almost exclusively on training and competing at 400 metres, it would be another four years before I finally broke that world record, at the 1999 World Championships in Seville, Spain, running 43.18 in the final.

TO EACH HIS OWN

Clearly it is a long and difficult process of study, self-discovery and trial and error to break a world record or even to set a personal best. Since 2004 I have been working with American 400-metre runner Jeremy Wariner. Jeremy succeeded me as Olympic champion in 2004. He ran 44 seconds flat in that race to take the gold, and since that time he has run several sub-44-second 400-metre races and has come within 27 hundredths of a second of breaking my world record. Jeremy has been coached throughout his career by Clyde Hart, who coached me during mine. I am Jeremy's agent and mentor. My former training partner Deon, a world-class 400-metre runner himself in the nineties, works for my management company and travels around the world with Jeremy, handling logistics and putting him through his workouts when Clyde isn't there. Between Clyde, Deon and myself Jeremy is surrounded by probably more 400-metre training expertise and race knowledge than anyone else in the world. Even so, after seven years of trying, Jeremy, undoubtedly the second best and second most consistent 400-metre sprinter in the history of the event, has not yet broken the world record. That is not due to a lack of talent. We cannot simply have Jeremy do everything that I did in my training and assume that will bring him the same level of success.

Each athlete is different. I obviously had the talent to break the 400-metre world record, and so does Jeremy. But he will have to do it differently. Where I was always the fastest 400-metre runner on the track, due to being a world record 200-metre runner with tremendous speed, Jeremy is not nearly as fast as I was. But Jeremy has uniquely superior speed endurance, meaning that he can get to race pace and hold that high level of speed for a very long time without being affected by fatigue. That is a huge advantage for a

400-metre sprinter. So Jeremy has to train differently and run the race differently. Of course there are more similarities between us and our training programmes and race strategies than there are differences. But at this level it is the differences – and understanding those differences – that will determine whether Jeremy breaks my world record or finishes his career with me always being able to say, 'You couldn't get me!'

I really hope, however, that he's eventually the one doing the teasing. People should not have been surprised in 2008 to find that I wasn't sad or disappointed when Usain Bolt broke my 200 record, since it was well known that since 2004 I've been trying to help Jeremy to break my 400 record. The pride that I feel in breaking both records comes not from being able to say today that I am still the world-record holder, but rather from knowing all the work behind those accomplishments. And that is the joy I get now in working with Jeremy and Coach to try and figure out the right customised training programme and race strategy that will help Jeremy break the world record, and watching Jeremy do his part.

STRATEGIC THINKING

We are now in an era of sport when there is so much money and sport is so powerful and such a part of our society, it's no longer enough to be one of the most physically gifted athletes or even a physically gifted athlete who works hard. The Olympic legends, the athletes who have made history in one of the world's oldest sports championships and repeatedly dominated at the Olympic level, are those hardworking, physically superior athletes who have taken the time to learn and master their sport and even their mental condition. These athletes have an incredible mental grasp on strategy, technique, their competitors and themselves at a very detailed level. They are obsessed with learning and constantly think about strategy. They train physically for their sport every day, and then study their sport in their spare time.

And that requires staying power. As Sebastian Coe told me, there are thousands of hours tucked away behind the success of an Olympic champion. That ability to stay the course, to accept that it doesn't happen overnight, is critical. 'This is the big problem now. A lot of young people live in a world that is very counter-culture to that. Reality television creates heroes over six hours. You and I weren't created in six years,' Seb told me. 'If we're honest about it, we probably weren't created within a decade. I started in track and field at 11 or 12. I didn't get to a Games until I was 23. By any stretch of the imagination, that is a long apprenticeship. Sport allows you to put that into perspective. It helps you pick when you need to be tactical, but at the same time always having that strategic view that this is an important year, but next year is a very important year, and the year after that might be even more important. So it helps you prioritise.'

Hurdler Sally Gunnell told me that she thinks that as much as 70 per cent of athletic success involves the mind. 'It's finding the tools, understanding yourself, putting yourself in situations and learning about yourself,' she says. I completely agree. It takes a lot to prepare, and the work doesn't just happen on the track, in the pool, on the court or field or in the weight room. You have to spend a lot of time thinking and planning how to be successful.

In addition, you also have to learn to manage those inevitable pre-competition negative thoughts. It's not enough to say, 'Don't think negative thoughts.' You have to replace those thoughts with something else. I'll never forget the time when I was in a call room at the 1996 Games and Frankie Fredericks walked past me. I immediately started to think about all the times we'd run against one another. It was always tough against him. As soon as I became aware of that train of thought, I stopped myself and began to visualise myself running the race.

That was my automatic default response. I would hear the gun go off in my head and start going through my paces. Then I'd visualise the whole thing again. I think being somewhat quiet and reserved helped me. In situations where the pressure was on, I had a distinct advantage because I could revert to my natural tendency to go inside my own mind. Instead of being distracted by exterior people or events, I focused on running a perfect race in my head.

That mindset doesn't just take place during competition. A number of the Olympian champions I interviewed told me that whether they were training, relaxing or working on hobbies, they thought about, planned and visualised themselves executing a winning performance. In short, they lived, ate, drank and breathed their sport, which is what's required in order to be a great Olympic athlete. Throughout my career, any time I wasn't doing something that required my full attention my mind defaulted back to thinking about and visualising races. Several times a day, I would automatically imagine the gun going off and myself contending with a different scenario each time I ran.

That's the kind of strategic positive thinking that works. The 200 sprint, for example, is so technical that you have to develop a race strategy before the gun goes off and then stick to that. It's all in the preparation. The 400, on the other hand, demands a completely different approach. I'd make all kinds of adjustments in that race, based on what other people were doing or how I'd gone through a particular phase of the race. Running through the options in my mind before I ever hit the track was critical.

Throughout her career Sally Gunnell also visualised herself reacting differently depending on how the race unfolded. She ran her races so often in her mind that when she had to race with a cold during the World Championships in 1993 she was able to go on to autopilot. 'With the hurdles, I always knew American Sandra Farmer-Patrick would be way ahead at 200. I also knew that if I was coming off the eighth hurdle in the lead, it was mine. So I had to work with that in my mind.' Sally did that so often that for a brief moment she wasn't sure whether the gold medal she had just won despite not feeling up to par physically was real or imagined. 'I remember crossing the finish line and thinking, "Am I in a dream or has that really happened?" Because I'd done it so many times in my mind!'

MENTAL GAMES

THE PRESSURE OF SUCCESS

Winning, however, comes with its own burden in the shape of unrelenting pressure that intensifies the better you get. To succeed, you have to learn to live with that. After I had won Olympic gold in the 1996 Atlanta Games and broken the world record in the 200 metres, Frankie, who finished second and ran very fast as well, was asked during the post-race press conference whether the pressure had gotten to him. He had been favoured because I was doubling in the 200 metres and 400 metres, which meant that by the time I reached the 200-metre finals I had already run four rounds of the 400 and three rounds of the 200. Frankie was doubling only in the traditional 100-metre/200-metre double. Running 100-metre races instead of 400-metre races certainly gave him an advantage. Additionally, the 100 metres is the first event held at the Olympics in track and field and the 200 metres falls at the end, so Frankie had four days of rest between the final of the 100 metres and the preliminaries of the 200 metres. I had one day between the 400 metres final and the 200 metres preliminaries. Expectations that he would win gold in the 200 were further fuelled by the fact that he had beaten me during a tune-up race in Oslo the month before. But of course he did not win Olympic gold and I did. After the race he told the media that he felt that he would have had a better chance of being victorious had he not become the favourite. That shocked me. Until that point I always thought that every competitor wanted to be the favourite, because I always did.

Unlike many of the other athletes I interviewed for this book, Chris Hoy has not retired, so his battle with pressure isn't over. Not only does he want to win in front of the British home crowd in 2012, he wants to bring home gold in all three of his events. Luckily, as the top man to beat in cycling, Chris is used to dealing with that level of expectation. 'It's almost like you're in a no-win situation,' he told me. 'If you win, people expect it and go, "That's what you should be doing." If you think about it that way, it's a huge amount of pressure. But what I think about now is that nothing can take away my past performances. Nothing can take away from the gold medals at Beijing, the gold medal at Athens, the world championships. So I don't think about the outcomes; I only think about performance.'

Chris and I discussed how competing in front of a home crowd automatically brings with it a tremendous amount of pressure. I certainly felt that in Atlanta, and Ian Thorpe, despite coming back from a broken ankle, felt that as the favourite in Sydney during the 2000 Olympics. But with that pressure of being the favourite also comes incredible opportunity. As I experienced, you can choose to focus on the pressure or on the support you get from the home crowd.

Either way, you still have to contend with self-imposed pressure. By aiming to duplicate his Beijing achievement of winning gold in all three of his events, Chris Hoy could effectively paralyse himself. But I get the sense that he knows just how to contend with and channel that internal pressure, especially since one of those events will be a team effort only partially within his control.

'Ultimately, you can't predict medals because you don't know what your rivals are going to be like. You can produce the best ride of your life and get second. Or you could produce a sub-standard ride and still win. It just depends on your competition,' Hoy concluded. 'All I know is my goal is to be the best prepared that I've ever been in my career. I want to go up to the start line in London in the best shape of my life. That simple goal takes away all the other distractions and brings it back to yourself. You say, "You know what, if someone beats me, then it's because they deserve it. But it won't be because I didn't train hard enough or prepare properly. I want to leave no stones unturned."'

All champions develop their own very personal way of dealing with such enormous expectation from themselves or others. Rebecca Adlington doesn't feel fear when she races, even when she's behind. While competing in Beijing, she somehow found the physical and mental strength to pull out the gold after trailing in seventh place. Competition may not be a problem for Rebecca, but the expectations put on her after she won in Beijing proved to be another matter. 'People don't know swimming very well. It's just not a big sport,' she told me. 'All they know about swimming is Phelps, and Phelps wins everything. They just think I'm kind of like that, but Phelps is one of those rare human beings who are unbelievable.' Still, sidestepping those expectations, however unrealistic, proved difficult. 'When I went to the Worlds in '09, I couldn't handle the pressure of feeling that I had to repeat my performance in Beijing.'

The reaction to her coming in third instead of winning at the World Championships, even though she had swum a personal best, proved even more difficult to handle. 'I've never been one to want attention. So I found it really weird that everyone was looking at me and everyone was talking about it. I didn't appreciate that even when I lost people would still talk about it. I'd often see stuff across the newspapers about it. I didn't expect that and I didn't know how to handle it.'

Recognising that she had begun to put 'loads of pressure' on herself to win simply because of others' expectations, she began seeing a sports psychologist. 'He's helped me so much to realise what works for me,' she told me. 'I expect so much of myself all of the time. I know I can do better. Then it's me that makes the pressure worse rather than other people. My friends and family, they're not mad at me if I swim bad. It's because I am disappointed, not for any other reason. Same with all the sponsors and the media and all that sort. People have been really nice. Even after the Europeans when I didn't swim very well in the 800, so many people on Twitter and Facebook left so many nice messages. I got to the point where I was like, hold on, I'm putting all this pressure on myself for absolutely no reason.

'Last year, 2010, was different to a normal year because I had two major competition trials – Commonwealths and Europeans. It was a chance to go in and relax and not put so much pressure on. I'm learning ways now that help me to relax and not think about the outcome so much. I'm more focused on the process and the journey and going through the race rather than the outcome before I've even swum it. Before my races I think, "I can do this," rather than "I should win this." I think about my prior successes and focus on what I've done in training. "I do this race in the pool every single day," I tell myself. "It's all water, it's just a pool. If I can do it there, I can do it here."' Perhaps most importantly, she has learned to stop thinking of Beijing as a perfect experience that she has to duplicate.

Rebecca is far from being the only athlete who has had to deal with the pressure of sudden success. 'We are never catapulted into the limelight in the way most people think we are,' Sebastian Coe told me. 'There's 10,000 hours behind that.' But sometimes, even 10,000 hours doesn't seem like enough when people start pinning their Olympic hopes on you, a feeling Seb knows all too well. 'In 1978, I'd nicked a bronze medal in a European championship. I'd broken a British record. Halfway through 1979 and I'd broken the 800, the 1500 and the mile within 41 days. Somewhere in the middle, journalists were basically hanging medals around my neck and saying, "He's broken the world record. Of course he's going to win the Olympics." And God help you if you don't perform up to expectation.'

Clearly, even those of us who enjoy – and court – pressure have to learn how to handle it. And nowhere is the pressure more intense than at a home Olympic Games. Pull it off, and you make history. Just as Atlanta was the defining moment of my career, Sydney was the defining moment of Cathy Freeman's when she competed in the 2000 Sydney

Games in front of her home crowd. I remember her race, in part because no one was paying any attention to the race I was running. It was almost as if we weren't even there.

'We're a small country,' she countered when I mentioned that during our interview. 'We don't have many successes in track and field.'

Cathy, of course, was the notable exception. She wasn't just good, she was great. She wasn't just expected to medal, she was expected to win. And this scorching spotlight of expectation fell on to a young woman who has never been one to care for being the centre of attention or in the lime-light. 'I'm very happy with my own company,' she told me. 'I'm not one of these people who needs to be with people all the time.'

So how did she cope? 'I don't take myself all that seri-ously,' she said. 'You've got to have the ability to laugh at yourself. It's a really important way of coping with little setbacks or frustrations or pressure or drama and conflict. I've always been determined to live my life the way I want to live it. I've always been clear on the sort of person I am and the person I want to be, and the person I don't want to be. I can feel shifts within myself sometimes where there is an opportunity to change, but I think I've got pretty good instincts. I back my judgement. I trust in who I am. That's why I'm always grounded and I always feel safe wherever I go and whoever I'm with, because I know that within myself is everything I will ever need. I don't feel like I've got to buy into what other people see in me. At the end of the day, so many performers talk about how the only pressure that really matters is the pressure we place on ourselves, anyway. That's exactly what I was like, as well. It was that tunnel vision. All that I see is all *I* see.'

During the lead-up to those same Sydney Olympics, Australia's Ian Thorpe had been so successful that, in his words, 'It was almost assumed that I'd win.' This at a home Olympics in a country as fanatical about swimming as other countries are about football. And let's not forget that Ian at the time was just 17 years old and was recovering from a broken ankle. Instead of providing him with an excuse, 'A new pressure was created, because I had to get back into shape.' Indeed, since he didn't want his competitors to think that if they just pushed a little harder they might have a chance due to Ian's injury, he tried to keep the whole thing quiet. 'It was a stupid thing to think that I'd be able to do it. But also, in my own mind, I didn't want this to be something that was staring down at me. So as soon as I broke my ankle, everyone else was more concerned than me. I just looked at it as being another obstacle that when I stood behind the blocks I knew what I'd been through and that that was going to add to my performance.'

Ian dealt with the multi-faceted stress and monster expectation by not allowing himself to really grasp just how much pressure he was under. That worked for him, even though the Olympic experience itself threatened to derail him. 'I had received advice from other athletes who said, "No matter what you've experienced, until you get to the Olympic Games you haven't experienced anything." Do you know what? It's really quite true. But it's also false.

'I tried very hard to separate the competition from the Olympics and what goes on with an Olympics. It's really different to any other competition. I tried to separate it and tried to just be a Zen master about this whole thing and just go into competition. But I had a terrible swim. I didn't struggle and qualified fastest for the final, but it came at a higher cost than I was used to. So I had all these doubts right before the race. Australia hadn't won at this stage, which adds more expectation. But people almost innocently assumed that I'd win without thinking about what I might be struggling with.

'Then they announced my name. I was used to getting big cheers when I stood on the blocks right before the start of a race, but I hadn't anticipated the big roar from the crowd. I couldn't do anything but smile. That moment interrupted my negative thoughts and helped allow a little bit of humanity into what I was trying to do. When they moved past my lane to announce the next person, I was in game mode. I started to relax even more into myself, to go to what I knew and to become dangerously relaxed. That was the turning point for me. I was ready to compete and I was ready to win.'

Despite his youth and the relentless pressure he was under, Ian went on to deliver three golds and two silvers. Many athletes, however, when confronting immense pressure will damage their chances by playing mental games with themselves. These athletes will try to convince themselves that this isn't so important and that it's just another competition. That doesn't work because it's not reality, and at some point – and possibly the worst point, just before the start of the competition – that reality comes back and slaps them right in the face. Then panic ensues.

Other athletes will start making excuses before the competition even starts in an effort to manage expectations. At this point the athlete has stopped believing in himself. He still hopes that he can do well and deliver, but without belief it is almost impossible. You can't have it both ways. Athletes attempt to hedge their bets, but that doesn't work in a high-stakes game, and the Olympics is a high-stakes game. You're either all in or you're out. I actually set the expectations bar so high that at times it wasn't enough for me to just win. I had to win by a margin so great that the race wouldn't be close.

Usain Bolt will have this same problem. He has set the bar so high by breaking world records in his last two championships and at such a young age that fans expect more and more. He is by far the most famous person in his small country. When he arrives in London for the 2012 Olympics, back in Jamaica the entire country will be watching his every move.

During the Beijing Games in 2008, when Usain competed and broke world records en route to winning gold in the 100 metres, the 200 metres and the 4 x 100m relay, the country of Jamaica came to a standstill. There were huge television monitors in the middle of Kingston, with mobs of people standing in the streets to watch and celebrating wildly after his victory. He is a great source of pride for Jamaicans, not only living in Jamaica but all around the world. The large population of Jamaicans living in London will be supporting Usain in 2012 and hoping for not only victories from him but more world-record-setting performances. Preparing mentally for this will prove even more difficult than getting ready physically. It's all in how he balances his own approach to the challenge. While there are huge expectations of him and he is well aware of this, he will have to focus on his own goals and not the expectations of his many supporters. The key is not to try to ignore those expectations or pretend they are not there, but to acknowledge they exist and develop a plan to deal with them while you focus on your own goals.

LOSING HURTS BUT IT DOESN'T KILL YOU

Some athletes try to convince themselves that neither the competition nor whether they win or lose really matters. This is huge mistake. During my career I simply refused to dwell on the possibility, choosing instead to focus on what I need to do to win the race.

Like every top athlete, I hate to lose. But I wasn't scared of losing. My coach used to say, 'We're not afraid to run against anyone, they can't eat us.' This was his way of reminding me that the competitors I lined up against weren't monsters, they were just athletes. There was no reason to be afraid. If they beat us, we would learn from it, line up against them next time and do better.

That doesn't mean that you accept those losses. You can't be okay with losing or performing below what you think you're capable of. Hating to lose, however, often transforms itself into being afraid to lose. As a result, the focus shifts from offence to defence. 'Yeah, I could win, but I am so afraid of losing that I'd rather focus on trying not to lose rather than trying to win.' Or athletes, especially those who already have huge contracts negotiated on the basis of their potential, simply shield themselves from being in a position to lose.

These days, however, there is such desperation from countries to find the next Olympic medallist and from sports teams and clubs and sportswear companies to find the next star that athletes are identified very early on the strength of their potential alone. Instead of learning to question themselves, they're rewarded with significant contracts, attention and even endorsement opportunities before they have proved themselves. As a result of being told for so long that they have the talent and that they are that good, they wind up thinking that they're entitled to Olympic success.

This has become a particularly acute problem in the UK, where athletes are insulated against loss and rewarded for mediocrity and 'potential'. I've experienced how the Brits take care of their athletes, both as a journalist and as an athlete. When I was competing as a 200- and 400-metre runner, when I would come to the UK to compete, the promoter of the UK events, Andy Norman, would say to me, 'Hey, Michael, we want you to come and run here.' I'd say, 'Okay, I want to run a 400.' Then they'd say, 'Nope, you can't run a 400. I've got Roger Black in the 400 and you can't be beating him on home soil. I will pay you more to run the 200.' And sometimes I'd say, 'Okay, I'm going to come to London. I want to run the 200.' This time they'd say, 'No, John Regis is going to run the 200. We can't have you beating him on home soil. We'll pay you more to run the 400.'

These were great athletes, world champions and Olympic medallists. They probably didn't even know they were receiving this type of protection and would probably have been disappointed if they had known it was being provided to them. Those athletes wanted to be the best in the world and take on the best, whether the best came to their country or if they had to go outside the UK to compete. But today's British athletes take that kind of protection and no longer venture abroad. Ironically, instead of creating more champions, taking care of them has stripped the country's current athletes of a lot of their hunger. As a result, they end up not competing as much, or they don't compete against their main competition. And when they do lose, they look for people to blame instead of focusing on what else they need to do in order to win.

Of course, even world-class champions will question their readiness, but only to a certain point, as Cathy Freeman confirmed. 'I was always at a point where you kind of look over your shoulder and can't help but ask yourself, even on a subconscious level, "Have I done enough work? Am I ready? Have I done everything I possibly can to get myself in the best shape possible physically?" Two weeks, a week, or a few days away from an Olympic Games or World Championships, you've really got to put your doubts aside and you've got to put your negative thoughts aside, and you've just got to focus on your strengths.'

ALL ABOUT ATTITUDE

Attitude, as much as anything, defines the successful competitor. 'I thrived on competition,' Cathy Freeman told me. 'I loved it. Any chance I got to race, I would be in there. As soon as I went to a competition, my focus was always to turn it on and get on with it and do the best I could.'

When you meet Cathy off the field, she's so grounded and so contemplative that it's hard to imagine her clicking into competition mode, especially since competitiveness is usually associated with someone with a much more aggressive personality. But for Cathy, competition on the track didn't mean beating her opponents as much as it meant tapping into the deepest part of her being in the best way she knew how. 'You and I both understand that our running was our voice,' she told me during our interview. 'It was the voice that was going to make people stand up and listen, even though that wasn't always the central intention. At the end of the day, it was always going to be *my* voice. I am pretty quiet and reserved. Even as a 12-year-old girl it was hard for people to ignore the fact that I had a natural running style, and it was really difficult for people to not create aspirations for me before I'd even realised them. But I was always going to be a runner from a young age, and running was always going to be my voice. It was this expression of who I was. It suited my personality perfectly, because

I'm definitely more of doer than a talker. You could see who I was through the running. I didn't need to say much.

'This means of expression meant that I could take my feelings, my deepest emotions, that energy and transform it into this physical performance. I was still grieving publicly for the loss of my father and my sister, and I've always felt the struggle for rights of my people out here in Australia. My parents, as recent as the sixties and seventies, had to get permission to go and spend time with their families for Christmas. I mean, behind that story is a pain that you carry. That always came out in my athletic performance. You add to that a hatred of losing and wanting to stand for something – to take that anger or intense emotion and transform it into something constructive – and you can become pretty unstoppable. I can't actually, really, articulate the intensity of those emotions, because words aren't there. They simply aren't enough, which is why I was such a competitive beast, Michael.'

I urge the athletes I work with to learn to embrace the kind of competitiveness that Cathy Freeman felt so deeply rather than the fear of losing or not performing as well as they want to. It's not about not wanting to lose. It's about wanting to win. Of course not every athlete can win every competition. But every athlete can win when it comes to personal performance. For example, there was a special point in my career in 1988 when I was a sophomore in college who hadn't been on any US teams. Suddenly I found myself racing against a guy named Emmit King, who was a world-class 100-metre runner, Calvin Smith, who was a

200-metre world champion and former world record holder, and a guy named Mel Lattany, who was a world-class runner at 100 and 200 metres. I wasn't world class yet. Far from it. So losing that race wouldn't have been a failure. The fact that I won that race was huge for me. Once I became the world champion, Olympic gold medallist, world record holder – the best in the world – any race I lost was going to be a failure.

During the 1996 Games, Nike had a controversial billboard campaign that, as per Nike's usual, pushed the envelope. Billboards all over Atlanta read, 'You don't win silver. You lose gold.' That was true for me, but it isn't for the majority of competitors. For some athletes, just making it to the Olympics is a victory.

Frankie Fredericks was a silver medallist in 1992 in the 100 and 200 metres. In 1996 he was the silver medallist in the 100 and 200 metres again. He got four silver medals. He doesn't have a gold medal. Could he have won? Who knows. In 1992 he lost the 100 metres to Linford Christie. Linford was a better athlete than Frankie was. In 1996 he lost the 100 metres to Donovan Bailey, but Donovan broke the world record in that race. Then, in the 200 metres, he lost to me. I also broke the world record in that race. So is that failure? No, that's success for him.

That same record would have been failure for me. I was expected to win gold. However, if I had trained with the notion of not losing the gold medals I was expected to win, I would have been lucky to end up with Fredericks's results. Because instead of focusing on what was possible and going all out to achieve what was possible, I would have been limited by the fear of not performing to the level of expectations of myself and others.

While the fear of losing is often paralysing, some athletes actually use it as motivation. Tanni Grey-Thompson told me, 'The fear of losing made me train really hard. I was terrified of being on the starting line and not having done everything I possibly could. I'm a bit of a control freak, and I wanted to feel as much in control as I possibly could. I felt a lot more in control if I knew I'd done everything I could possibly do and left nothing to chance.'

Sally Gunnell also admitted that she was so afraid of losing that she 'trained scared ... I trained bloody hard because I was scared of losing. I put so much pressure on myself.' In 1992 nobody expected Sally to even medal. 'I knew that I'd done everything and that I was going to win,' she recalls. But no one else did. That changed the following year when she entered the World Championships as an Olympic gold medallist. She dealt with the pressure of expectations by, in her words, force-feeding herself the notion that you don't become a bad athlete overnight. 'You know you're capable of winning. You're in the shape of your life. The only thing between you winning or not is this up here and you not believing in yourself. I didn't want that to be the reason why I had lost,' she said. 'I knew now what I was really capable of doing. I knew I could break world records. I knew I could win Worlds. I'd set it all out.'

Of course, some athletes seem to thrive on amplifying public expectations. Take Mark Spitz announcing to the world that he would win six Olympic gold medals at the 1972 Olympics. He had made the same prediction four years earlier, and only wound up with two team gold medals. This was to be his last Olympics. It was now or never.

Fortunately, the notion that he was winding up his competitive athletic career helped inspire his training and diminish his sense of pressure before that record-setting 1972 Olympics. 'For something that I loved, which is my sport, I really don't like working out. But starting from 4 September 1971, every single day was the last time that I was ever going to have to work out on that day. So, I was lightening the load,' he told me. He would tell himself, 'I'm going to make this workout special. I am going to make a deposit of some value and it's always going to be positive. For all the times in the past that I held back, I don't need to hold back any more because it's one brick off of that cart of responsibility that I've placed on my shoulders. Dammit, I'm going to make sure this is the best race. How do I be sure of that? Relive in my mind that image of what it was like to swim all those years before in every single race that felt easy.

'Every single day that I swam, I relied on that feeling of confidence. I said, I am embracing this; I *want* to swim this event. Every second, every stroke is going to be lighter, faster, quicker because I am that much closer to winning the gold medal. All I have to do is stay focused on exactly the same way I have always won against my competitors. Once I win that gold medal, because I am swimming in another event the next day, my God, I am better, I am faster, and the load is getting lighter, and the sense of responsibility is getting less. You know that your 100 metres and 200 metres, those races were different. You had different competitors and different situations. You had different angles. One you're going straight. One you're making a turn.

'You know that once you've got through with one of those events, all of that shit's out of your brain. It makes you a lot clearer for the next day. Even going from preliminaries to semi-finals, you become so much clearer. To me, I was going, it's no different. It's just another day in the office, but God, the load is getting lighter and my confidence is great. I didn't even concentrate on times. I just told myself, "If I swim my honest race, it's going to be fast." I didn't give a shit about times, because at the end of the day it's all about the gold medal. That just went along with the ride.'

Despite how daunting expectations of victory can be, even when they've been cultivated by the athletes themselves, many have clearly courted that kind of self-imposed pressure. For four years Steve Redgrave and his team-mate had told people that they were going to win a gold medal at the Atlanta Games. After all, they had won in Barcelona in the same boat. Besides, telling people that they would win gold helped motivate them to keep training as hard as they could. 'Then suddenly you get to that week and you're thinking this is it. It's what we do this week that makes the difference,' recalls Steve. 'I really struggled with the pressure in some ways ...The World Championships are nice, but they're just stepping stones towards the next Olympics. Suddenly you've got to deal with that expectation, with your own expectation at that particular time. The bits for me that were sheer hell were the last little bit of waiting around: that last two or three hours with butterflies in your stomach, thinking, "Why am I doing this? This is just awful. Why do I keep coming back to this? This is just dreadful." I was rowing then with Matt Benson, who would be curled up fast asleep in a ball an hour before we go. "How can he sleep at this time?" I'd wonder. Then you start thinking you're getting too nervous; you're going over the top and you're not going to get the best performance out of yourself because of the state you're getting yourself into.

'In some ways, I had to get myself into that state to be able to get a good performance, but it is very much a knife edge of being able to go off the other way. In the last hour or so I'd be laying around in the rest area sort of thinking through the tactics of the race and thinking – just go out and race; you've done so much for four years of hard graft. All the hours and sacrifice that you've put into this – just go out and race and get the best performance you possibly can and don't come back. And that's it. Then you go out there and do it.

'A few months later, you find yourself rowing up and down at Henley doing your training and you're thinking, "God, I said I was never going to do this again, but here I am! That was fun; it was really exciting at the Olympics." But in that moment it is the worst place in the world.'

Steve and I are different. As difficult as that moment is just before you have to go out and prove yourself in the Olympic arena, I love it. I dealt with that kind of pressure and elevated expectation by being in control at all times and by putting so much pressure on myself to deliver that the rest paled by comparison. That was especially true going into the 1996 Olympics. I was the face of those Games. The schedule had been changed to allow me to attempt a historic double. But I had put so much pressure on myself that I never focused on the external pressure. It just didn't matter.

6.

NO SHORTCUTS

Unfortunately, the desire to achieve results sometimes prompts athletes into taking shortcuts. In other words, they cheat.

Even as a kid, I knew that was wrong. When I was ten years old, as part of physical education in school, we would periodically do what was called a cross-country run across the fields of our school and around the park. We probably covered a distance of about 800 metres, but at the time it seemed like a long way to me. It probably seemed even longer because I was never able to come in first. Although I'd start out in first place, two of the kids in my class would always turn around before they reached the specified turn-around point. The other kids didn't care if they were cheating, but I did because I wanted to win. I'd run faster to try to catch them, but the advantage they'd gained by cheating always proved too great to overcome.

That was one of my first experiences with people cheating, and the whole idea that the competition wasn't fair bothered me. It never once entered my mind to turn around early like they did in order to even out the competition. I just had been taught by my parents to do the right thing.

My parents reinforced the message I'd gotten early on about cheating when I was 14 years old. They had always been very strict when it came to education, and would come down hard on me if I didn't do well. I did okay in school, but not great. I knew how to do the work and I was certainly capable of doing the work. Somehow, however, I just didn't consistently get it done – at least not on time. Once, when I got a pretty bad grade as a result, I tried to alter it. My sister, who was seven years older than me, discovered that I had changed the grade and made me tell my parents what I had done.

I was scared to death of what my father would do, since he routinely punished my siblings and me with whippings after a stern talking-to about why what we had done was wrong. My father was a very tough man and very tough on me, but he rarely showed his anger. In fact I can't remember him ever showing anger. He just wanted to make sure we learned our lesson. But when I told him that I had changed my grade, he simply told me that he was very disappointed in me and said a few things about trust. That was it.

My father is a very smart man and knew exactly the effect this approach would have on me. I never tried to cheat at anything again. I would find out the hard way, however, that too many athletes, even at the Olympic level, don't share that level of ethics.

When Antonio Pettigrew burst on to the athletics scene at the US championships in 1989 as an unknown 400-metre runner, he won the event in an impressive 44.27 seconds. Antonio had attended a small college not known for athletics, so his performance was a shock to everyone. Two years later at the 1991 World Championships in Tokyo he became world champion at 400 metres and I became world champion at 200 metres. We would compete against one another many times over the next ten years.

In Tokyo, Antonio anchored the US 4 x 400m relay and, with a lead when he received the baton, it could be safely assumed that the world champion would not be caught. That was exactly what the US coach, Tom Tellez, assumed at the time he decided not to include me on the 4 x 400m relay team, even though I was ranked number one in the world. Kriss Akabusi of Great Britain, however, caught Antonio at the line. That remains the last time the US finished anything but first in a 4 x 400m relay at a major championship.

Antonio suffered major embarrassment from the defeat in the 4 x 400. The embarrassment continued when I defeated him after he became the world champion and he had to settle for a number two world ranking. He struggled in his career from that point and didn't make another US team for several years. Despite a reputation as a weak competitor, in 1997 he started to make a comeback. Over the next few years he went on to make US teams, including the 2000 Olympic 4 x 400 team, which I anchored.

GOLD RUSH

In May 2008, eight years after we had won that race, Antonio announced that he had used performance-enhancing drugs. Until then I had held great respect for his mature and serious approach to the sport. I considered him a friend. Although our friendship didn't extend past the track, we saw one another at competitions and talked often. To find that someone I liked and respected, someone I'd talked with about drugs in the sport, had himself used drugs disappointed me. It also made me feel naïve, since during the years of the Balco drug scandals I had consistently defended the sport, stating that the situation was not as bad as the media were making it out to be.

TAKING A STAND

I have always stood against performance-enhancing drugs. Because of that categorical stance, I made the decision to immediately return the gold medal I had won as a part of that Olympic relay team. Since my retirement in 2001, I had been a five-time Olympic gold medallist. Suddenly, I was downgraded to a four-time Olympic gold medallist. Since then, every time I am introduced as a four-time Olympic gold medallist I feel anger towards Antonio. My anger remains as potent today as it was when I saw him a few months after his admission and two days after I had actually returned the medal. I'm sure he had read about my disappointment and my decision to return the medal, and I felt he should have had something to say to me. But he never did.

NO SHORTCUTS

I have often wondered what it is like for those athletes who have accomplished great things and made their family and friends and all associated with them very proud, only to be exposed later as drug cheats. How do you move on with your life after suffering such embarrassment and inflicting such grief on all those people who have supported you? I'm sure that it has to be extremely difficult. We will never know what Antonio Pettigrew experienced on that front. We do know, however, that in August 2010 he apparently took his own life, leaving his wife and young son without a husband and father. The fact that, at the time of his death, he appeared to be doing a good job and was making a positive impact on the lives of young people as an assistant coach at the University of North Carolina makes the event even sadder, especially since, due to his choice to use performance-enhancing drugs, most people will only remember him as a drug cheat.

I didn't really begin to understand what performance-enhancing drugs were all about until Ben Johnson tested positive for drugs in 1988 in Seoul. At the time I was not a big Carl Lewis fan and I liked Ben's style. In contrast to Carl's flamboyance, Ben was fairly quiet and confident. I remember watching the big showdown between the two that year. Even at that time I scrutinised athletes' body language. Ben's businesslike demeanour stated plainly that he knew he would win. Right then, I knew that Carl would lose.

My college room-mate and I bet on the race. I took Ben, who of course won it running away. Two days later as I was heading out of my apartment to training, the news came over the television that Ben had tested positive. I was as amazed as I was disillusioned.

HOW IT HAPPENS

During all my 11 years as a professional runner and the four years at university before that, not a single person ever approached me about using drugs. That's due in part to my coach, Clyde Hart, one of the most honest and honourable men I've ever known.

There are basically two ways people end up using performance-enhancing drugs. Either they go out on their own and they seek it, or the coach goes out and seeks it for them. I wasn't going to go out and seek anything like that. I also feel confident that, had I had a different coach – one who suggested something that wasn't right – I would have run away from there as fast as possible. The fact that Clyde was my coach insulated me even more from steroid use. He would never have suggested anything like that, because he has a strong stance against not just performance-enhancing drugs but anything that's against the rules. Having grown up with my parents, who were all about doing the right thing and who believed that only hard work would get you where you wanted to go, I moved to being with Clyde who said the exact same thing.

I get asked all the time about whether I was approached about using performance-enhancing drugs. Nobody approaches you about that, unless it's your coach. No stranger or anyone else comes to you and says, 'Hey, you know what? You should use this. It'll make you faster.' Performance-enhancing drug use happens when athletes dream of being a champion or making it to the Olympics, but despite working super hard it's just not happening for them. They start wondering, 'Why am I not having success?' Then they start thinking, 'Maybe I can get a little help.'

Most of the time the athletes try to justify using performance-enhancing drugs by saying that everyone else is doing it, so they have to as well in order to level the playing field and survive in the sport. I used to believe this was a lot of crap, but the Balco scandal revealed that many of the athletes using steroids were being supplied by the same source. The last person you can trust to be quiet about something like that is the person helping you to cheat.

Doping has long been an issue in sport, but over the last decade or so it has become a huge problem with various sports and in particular with athletics, the premier sport of the Olympics. As a result, there is a perception among the public that all sports are rife with drug use. But most people don't take into account that many athletes, in fact the majority, choose not to use performance-enhancing drugs. There are many reasons why. For starters, there is fear of getting caught. Most people don't know it, but track and field athletes are some of the most tested in the world.

I was tested over 125 times during my university and professional career. Track and field athletes are subject to mandatory testing at championships where most, if not all, of the finalists are tested. In invitational professional competitions around the world, random testing of athletes takes place, so athletes have no idea if they will be tested or not, and are only informed after they finish the race if they have been selected, because which athletes are to be tested is determined by place. So the second and fifth place finishers in the 100 metres may be selected for testing, while the first and seventh place finishers may be selected in the 1500 metres. In addition, every athlete is subject to random out-of-competition drug testing. Under this programme athletes must continuously update what is called a 'whereabouts' form, so that they can be subject to surprise testing at any time on any day. That may take place while they are training, relaxing at home, or in a hotel the day before a competition away from home. Under this system, the tester shows up with no advance notice and announces to the athlete that he has been selected for random out-of-competition testing. The tester does not then leave that athlete until the athlete produces a urine sample for testing.

Athletes who test positive suffer embarrassment, the potential loss of sponsors, and the potential ban from participating in the sport they love. Many high-profile athletes have tested positive and suffered all of the above over the last several years. In the men's 100 metres alone, in addition to Olympic champion Justin Gatlin (who has always professed his innocence) and European champion Dwayne Chambers, Tim Montgomery, the former world record holder, was banned for two years after testifying that he received performance-enhancing drugs from Balco. During that same era, Marion Jones, perhaps the biggest star in the sport until Usain Bolt, was also banned, having admitted to using performance-enhancing drugs after being investigated as part of the Balco scandal. Jones was the 2000 Olympic 100-metre gold medallist and was forced to forfeit that medal. The second place finisher in that race, Greek sprinter Ekaterina Thanou, has not been upgraded to gold, however, because of her own doping-related controversy. She was charged with making false statements during an investigation into an accident in which she was alleged to have been trying to avoid a random out-of-competition drug test on the eve of the 2004 Olympic Games in Athens.

The athletes found to have taken banned substances serve as examples of what can happen to you if you decide to take the shortcut. Most of these athletes have not only suffered public humiliation and basically an end to their careers, they've also endured financial disaster in the shape of lost sponsorship and in many cases a dearth of invitations from the major international invitational competitions around the world. These trials and tribulations, which other athletes are well aware of, serve as a huge deterrent for many young athletes coming up in the sport.

With so many of the stars from 2000 to 2008 involved in drug scandals, it is no surprise that the public have come to believe that the majority of athletes are doping. I blame the media for this misapprehension. An athlete who cheats and is caught provides salacious headlines, and our current society is interested in that type of scandalous news. Unfortunately, the media always spotlight an athlete testing positive, playing up the scandal more than the athletic achievements of clean athletes.

It bothers me that the media will still seek out Ben Johnson, the most high-profile drug cheat in the history of sport, for his comments on today's drug issues or his conspiracy theories and continued denials about taking steroids in 1988 when he was busted. He obviously has no credibility and should not continue to be given a platform to attempt to gain sympathy, especially considering the damage he caused to the sport of athletics and the Olympic movement by continually saying that pretty much every athlete in Olympic sport uses performance-enhancing drugs and that this is the only way to achieve Olympic success. As a result, the public still believes that most athletes probably use drugs. But as is the case in society, most athletes obey the rules and do the right thing.

Another problem is the confusion and the lack of consistency across the different governing bodies and federations when it comes to defining and regulating banned substances. Each sport in each country has its own federation. In the UK that would be UK Athletics, while in the US it's USA Track and Field. Each country also has an Olympic Committee – the British Olympic Association (BOA) in Britain and the US Olympic Committee (USOC) in the US. The International Association of Athletics Federations (IAAF) is the international governing body of athletics, and the International Olympic Committee (IOC) is the global governing body of the Olympic Games and Olympic sports. If all of that wasn't enough, during the last ten years, in response to the rise in drug cheats, more organisations have become involved in the process of dealing with drug testing and drug cheats. The World Anti-Doping Agency (WADA) was founded in 1999, and in the US we have an independent drug testing agency, the US Anti-Doping Agency (USADA). Additionally there is the Court for Arbitration in Sport (CAS), an international governing body that hears cases and appeals of cases involving athletes and performance-enhancing drugs.

With that many organisations on the case, you would think there would no longer be a drug problem. But in some ways the involvement of all of these different organisations has caused more problems when it comes to dealing with those athletes who have tested positive for performance-enhancing drugs or have been charged with cheating. Inconsistency in the rules and in the interpretation of the rules causes many problems. Take British sprinter Dwayne Chambers, who received a two-year ban in 2003 for testing positive for the substance THG. Chambers's two-year ban was handed to him by a UK Athletics tribunal that decided that THG was chemically or pharmalogically related to a substance on the IAAF's banned list of drugs. There was inconsistency from the beginning. Although the IAAF didn't specifically have THG on its banned list, when UK Athletics banned Chambers for two years the IAAF supported that ban. The BOA banned Chambers for life, citing its rule that if an athlete tests positive for a performance-enhancing drug that athlete can never be part of a British Olympic team ever again. That means that after Chambers served his two years he was free to compete again and represent himself in international invitational competitions, and even represent Great Britain in IAAF World Championship competitions, but he still cannot represent his country in the Olympics. In contrast, American sprinter and 2004 100-metre and 200-metre Olympic champion Justin Gatlin, who received a four-year ban in 2006 after testing positive for a substance believed to be testosterone, is now eligible to compete and represent his country for any team that he can make, because the USOC rules don't bar athletes for life. In fact, Great Britain is the only country that bans athletes testing positive for life.

It doesn't stop there. The IOC instituted a rule stipulating that any athlete who tests positive for performance-enhancing drugs and is banned for over six months will miss an Olympics. Since the Olympics take place every four years, this can mean that an athlete who receives a two-year ban from his federation will miss competing in an Olympics even if the Games take place after the ban is over. That ruling is being challenged by athletes, and so far the Court for Arbitration in Sport (CAS) has indicated that it agrees with the athletes due to the IOC's rule effectively being double jeopardy.

Of course, for every champion who has tested positive, there are several who have had long and successful careers without any positive tests or scandal. Allison Felix, two-time 200-metre world champion, Veronica Campbell, two-time Olympic 200-metre champion, Tyson Gay, the former 100- and 200-metre world champion, and Jeremy Wariner, the former 400-metre world and Olympic champion, among many others comprise the current group of great athletes who over the last seven years have had no drug scandals associated with their names while winning championship medals and challenging the times of the previous generation who almost destroyed the sport.

THE FUTURE OF PERFORMANCE-ENHANCING DRUG USE

As much as the IOC's doping policy and the creation of WADA are good efforts in the fight against drug cheats, there is still cause for concern about the future of cheating in sports. Steroids and other performance-enhancing drugs have been used by athletes for a very long time. Over the last few decades before the creation of organisations like WADA and USADA, drug cheats had gotten ahead of the testers and anti-doping organisations. The whole Balco scandal was discovered only after a coach sent a syringe to the USADA, which uncovered a doping regimen created for many athletes across athletics, baseball and American football based on two designer steroids called 'the cream' and 'the clear', which had been created specifically to be undetectable to the testers. In fact, two of the biggest Olympic sports athletes to be banned as a result of the Balco scandal, Marion Jones and Tim Montgomery, never actually tested positive even though they were both tested many times. They were both banned after admitting under evidence-inducing pressure to taking the drugs.

The future of drug cheating could take on many forms, from other designer steroids and performance enhancers created specifically to be undetectable, to existing drugs intended for medical use that may be discovered to aid in athletic performance before they're identified by the anti-doping agencies and placed on the banned list as performance enhancers.

You have to wonder about who sits around and invents the drugs for athletic performance enhancement and why. Most people automatically assume that because of the money and glory associated with sporting success it's a no-brainer that people spend time, money and energy developing these drugs. But the drug cheat athlete market is very small and the cost to develop some of these drugs is enormous. So that's not the typical scenario. What actually happens is that most of these drugs are not invented for the purpose of aiding athlete performance. They are invented by pharmaceutical companies either to cure patients suffering from disease or other medical issues or else to improve their quality of life.

It costs millions and millions of dollars to develop these drugs, test them and get them approved by the national drug agencies like the Federal Drug Administration, or FDA, in America before they can finally be manufactured and taken to the market. But those drugs, which are intended to be sold only through doctors' prescriptions, are often identified early on by rogue scientists, perhaps even those involved in the process of testing and developing these drugs and procedures, as potential athletic performance enhancers.

One such process that has recently been identified as a potentially huge problem in the future fight against drug cheats in sport is gene doping. The ethical and primary purpose of gene therapy, which was discovered in the 1970s, is to treat disease by manipulating the underlying genes. The idea of gene doping in athletes comes from research done to treat muscle-wasting diseases with gene therapy in order to re-grow or enhance those muscles. The fear is that athletes could also be treated to grow already healthy muscles to be bigger and stronger. WADA has already asked scientists to help find ways to prevent gene therapy from becoming the next big thing in doping.

It's unrealistic to think that some day we won't have drug cheats. To me sport is just a small microcosm of society. You have good and bad people in sport as you do in society. There are always people in society who will take the short-cut. That is why we will always have law enforcement. The same is true in sport. There will always be people who will take the shortcut, and so we will always need to police athletics with the help of anti-doping agencies and rules. As a result, unfortunately, certain levels of achievement – and certain athletes – automatically come under suspicion.

In no sport is that truer than in sprinting, which requires strength and power – qualities that can be enhanced by taking drugs like anabolic steroids and human growth hormone that increase muscle growth. Because of that, the sport has been blighted by cheats. Too many times, the fastest man and woman in the world have let us all down. And the cheating has become more sophisticated, with scientists developing designer drugs – drugs specifically designed to improve physical performance and be undetectable. Had Ben Johnson been taking the designer drug THG, and not a drug developed to treat anaemia, he would probably never have been caught.

The World Anti-Doping Agency is trying to keep pace with the drug cheats. Testing is now more widespread, high-tech, done both in and out of competition, and random. Still, people who no longer believe what they see are quick to question Usain Bolt's recent achievements. That Usain has shown a steady upward progression since his young days is a good sign. Like me, he has always been very fast and has just gotten faster. Of course, that never stopped people from saying that I took drugs. He has suffered the same accusations.

'How do you answer those people who say, "Why should we believe that you're clean when you're running so fast?"' I asked him.

'That doesn't bother me because I understand where it's coming from,' he said. 'People have done so much over the years – breaking records, and then, all of the sudden, they're on drugs. It's a shame for the sport. I can't do nothing. All I got to do is keep on running fast, keep on getting tested. I just got to keep doing what I do.'

Those assumptions are exactly what Ian Thorpe hates about performance-enhancing drug use. 'When you see an extraordinary performance, the first thing that you should think of is what an extraordinary performance,' he told me. 'You shouldn't come to a conclusion where you go, "Oh, they must be taking something." That is the biggest risk that we have to the sport in maintaining its integrity. Whatever costs we may have in the short term is far outweighed by the benefit of being completely transparent about it in the long term.'

This is especially true in the Olympics, where the media and fans become especially outraged by athletes testing positive for banned substances. 'I love this,' Ian added. 'We hold Olympic athletes to a higher standard than any other athlete in society. We value Olympic sport so much that our level of expectation of those athletes who participate is higher than in other sports. If we look at the professional sports, especially in the US – we shouldn't just tie in the US – but looking at baseball and the NFL, I think what's happened is we look at these sports as entertainment. Entertainment in the sense of it's a programme that we watch at a certain time each week or when it's on if it's only available at a certain time of the year, and we watch it religiously. We watch it to be entertained. We are entertained not by the spectacle of the sport but what it means to us for our team and for us to feel like we're a part of that. We value our teams and we want to see them do well. We kind of overlook some indiscretions that we shouldn't, just because we feel like we're a part of it. Whereas an Olympic athlete becomes very unrelatable. It's from such a select bunch that you're actually an Olympian or Olympic champion that the performance comes from a purity in sport that people appreciate and value. But ... how it impacts when they lie, they don't see themselves as being that person. It's outside the realm of possibility for them. Whereas these local teams that you support, you feel like you're a part of them, like you know them. I think this is where we've kind of blurred this.'

'The Olympics is in such a strong position,' continues Ian, 'not only as a brand but for what it offers to people around the world in being able to say there's a different way. There's a moral way. And basically, we're doing the right thing. We're not perfect. We're doing the right thing. There's a lot that other sports could learn from us.'

As Ian says, 'Most people, when they win, they have done it the right way and they're clean.' The extreme minority of athletes who don't should stop and consider a few points.

There is a huge risk with using the drugs. There are potential known and unknown health problems that could occur as a result of using these drugs.

Despite the name, performance-enhancing drugs aren't guaranteed to make you perform better. Marion Jones ran faster and jumped further before she used drugs. Why? Because drugs can't deliver the self-belief that comes from training to the point where you know you're ready. If I did the work and became the best that I could be, the race was as good as won. I didn't worry about the competition.

7.

THE HEAT OF BATTLE

Not worrying about the competition doesn't mean I wasn't competitive. On the contrary. I've always prided myself on being a fierce competitor who was afraid to compete against no one. I ran against anyone at any time and took on all comers.

In my opinion no one should be intimidated or affected by another competitor. In fact, part of the reason I actually chose athletics instead of other sports was because I didn't want to be affected by the competitors. I wanted to run my own race. In track and field you cannot affect what another athlete is going to do. He has his lane, you have yours. He's going to run his race, and he's going to run as fast as he can, neither of which have anything to do with you. So why worry about what you can't control? That's why I only thought about what type of race I would run and how fast I would go.

Athletes tend to think far too much about their rivals, and that costs them time and focus. You need to know about them, as we shall see, but you don't need to think about how they're competing and compare yourself to them. But that's exactly what I did when I was competing in college. Most people would probably say this is normal and should be expected, but I felt it was weak of me to be thinking about my competitor and worrying about his condition and his results coming into a competition against me.

I remember losing a conference championship in 1988 to Joe DeLoach, who went on to win the gold medal in the 200 metres in Seoul later that year. We competed against one another quite often in college, so I'd studied him a lot. The day before and on the day of the competition I saw him a few times, and each time I saw him I would then start to think about him and how fast he had run a couple of weeks before. There were some other good athletes in the race as well, but I was focused on DeLoach. After losing to him in the 200-metre final I was riding back to our university on the bus with my team-mates, and on my mind was the fact that I had singled him out and spent so much of my time thinking about him when I should have been thinking about my own race. It also dawned on me that I was, to some degree, giving Joe an advantage by giving him so much respect.

I'm not saying that an athlete shouldn't respect his competitors, and I always did, but to single one of them out means putting him above the others. From that point on my approach was always that there are seven other athletes in the race and I don't care what their names are, what their results are, or who they are.

KNOW YOUR RIVALS

Of course, that was during the race itself. Before I ever got to the starting blocks, I had studied my competitors thoroughly. I knew everything about who I was running against – their strengths, their weaknesses, how they competed, their race strategies, even their body language. And I knew their results coming into the competition. I would use that knowledge to help me compete better against them as opposed to letting it worry me or put one athlete above any other.

Careful study of my competitors also reveals weaknesses to me that I could take advantage of. Ironically, although I never beat DeLoach during my college years, I never felt in all of our races as if he should beat me, because he seemed to be weak to me. Joe was a training partner of Carl Lewis's and competed for the University of Houston. He was extremely talented and very fast but not a tough competitor. Since we were both from Texas I had known of him since high school. I studied him quite a bit. Prior to races I would observe his reaction when he caught sight of me and I would think, 'I don't believe that he really believes he can beat me.' He did beat me each time in college, but after the race he always looked as if he felt like he had gotten lucky. I remember coming home from class to watch on television as

DeLoach ran the 200 metres in Seoul and beat Carl Lewis to win the gold medal. I noticed that even after winning the Olympic gold medal, the ultimate accomplishment of a track and field athlete's career, he had the same look on his face that he had after beating me at the conference championships in college. He looked as if he didn't believe that he should have won. After that I never lost to Joe DeLoach again, Joe never won another major championship and three years later he was retired from the sport.

Leroy Burrell was my next main competitor. He was also from the University of Houston, the same university as Joe DeLoach and Carl Lewis, and he also trained with the same group they did, the Santa Monica track club. Leroy was a great athlete, a 100-metre champion who held the world record for the event twice in his career. He was also a great long jumper and 200-metre runner. During my final year of college, we ran against one another a few times. The first time was at the conference championship where I had lost to DeLoach two years before. I ran a new personal best, although wind assisted, at 19.91 seconds, but I didn't win that race. Burrell won the race in 19.61 seconds. There was excessive wind, so it wasn't as close to a world record as the time would suggest. Even so there was no doubt that Leroy ran extremely fast that day and had the race of his life. Still, I believed I should have won that race.

It was my first 200-metre race of the season and in it I made a major mistake. I knew exactly what it was. Leroy was always a little bit overweight for his height as a sprinter, which helped him with power in the 100 metres but caused him to tire at the end of the 200 metres. His running technique would completely break down in the last 60 to 70 metres. I had also noticed when watching tapes of him in the 200 that he was very uncomfortable around the curve and would usually reserve energy until he came out of the curve and then make a big powerful surge with 100 metres to go. That type of sudden acceleration in the middle of the race, however, takes almost all of your remaining energy and so it's only good for 40 or 50 metres. I had neglected to plan for and capitalise on that opportunity.

When we squared off a couple of months later in Barcelona, Spain, I looked forward to exacting some revenge, just as I had twice earlier that year on Joe DeLoach. This was a big race, because he and I were the new and exciting young sprinters of 1990. Now that I knew how to compete against him, I was doubly excited to run against him again. I knew that if I ran fast from the start I would make him even more uncomfortable on the curve and he would be chasing me down the straight over the last 100 metres. I just had to have confidence that after a fast start I could hold him off. Sure enough, I beat him during that race and in every race that followed.

I raced against Leroy a few more times before he, like DeLoach, retired from the sport after only a five-year career. Leroy was probably one of the weakest competitors I had ever seen. He was so talented that twice in his career, once in 1991 and once in 1994, he broke the world record for the 100 metres, making him the fastest man in the world. But never during his entire career did he manage to win a gold medal at a major championship. I would watch him from the stands or on television when he ran the 100, and on the starting line just before the start of a race, and I could sense from looking at him then that he didn't want to be there. I could also sense that he didn't care at that moment if he won the race or not, he just wanted it to be over because the pressure was too much. And most of his race results proved that to be true.

Frankie Fredericks was the competitor that I had the most respect for. He was consistent, and although he was quiet and reserved he was a fierce competitor. I refer to him often throughout this book because I learned so much about myself from competing against him at 200 metres. He always brought out the best in me. I knew I had to be ready and I could make no mistakes against Frankie. He was quicker than I was, but not by much, and I was definitely stronger. What I learned in terms of strategy from watching and studying Frankie was that he would always press and tighten up if I was ahead of him after coming off the bend. So I used that knowledge to develop my strategy for competing against him and all of my competitors.

In the 400 metres I had to contend with Quincy Watts, the 1992 Olympic gold medallist and a very strong 400-metre runner. One of the first things I noticed from studying Watts was how strong he was. He was notorious for running fast times and then walking off the track looking as if he wasn't fatigued at all. When I started competing against Watts, everyone talked about how he would beat me and said that he was better than me at 400 metres because

I wasn't a true 400-metre runner. I welcomed the challenge. In the 1993 World Championships, Quincy was the defending Olympic gold medallist at the 400 metres and I had not won a 400 world championship. I had, however, already beaten him at the US championships. Talk about a huge build-up. I beat Quincy and he finished out of the medals.

He put his defeat down to the fact that his shoe had come apart at the end of the race, and the media seemed to be joining in and accepting that excuse, even though my record at that point against Quincy was 2–0. So in that same press conference I threw down the gauntlet and said, 'Okay, get your shoe fixed and I will see you in Brussels, Berlin and Zurich over the next two weeks.' He got new shoes and I beat him each time.

Although I never lost to Quincy, I had great respect for him. He was a tough and very confident competitor who never seemed to be intimidated by me or anyone else. I'm sure that when he said that his shoe caused him to lose the race to me at the 1993 World Championships he actually believed that. After being defeated by me during the next three races and over the rest of his career, he never used another excuse. He also never gave up, and continued to compete hard. I knew that because of his strength I had to run a more conservative race when racing Quincy. When balancing the need to run my strategy with the need to race against the competition, with Quincy in the race I needed to shift the balance more towards racing. I needed to be ready to make adjustments in the race to account for his strength.

My main 400-metre rival was Butch Reynolds, the world record holder at 400 metres until I broke his record. He had broken the world record in 1988, running 43.29 seconds. The first year I competed against him was 1990. He had been ranked number one in the world and was the dominant 400-metre runner to that point. We were represented by the same agent and so we travelled together. We would talk about the 400 quite a bit and we were good friends. Reynolds, however, would run the most inconsistent seasons of any 400-metre runner I'd ever seen. I wondered why, so I studied him as an athlete and competitor and listened to him carefully when we talked. That's when I figured out that Reynolds really didn't understand how to run fast. He didn't know why he had run fast when he did, and he didn't understand race strategy at all. He would employ different race strategies throughout the season and so each race was different.

Reynolds was suspended and banned for two years for steroid use after producing a positive urine sample. He maintained his innocence (and still does) and challenged the verdict in court. It was a huge case that kept the lawyers busy for years. It was later found that the testing procedures used for the urine had been flawed but the IAAF nonetheless upheld the ban. I've always been uncertain as to whether or not he used drugs. He never ran close to the time that he ran when he broke the world record, and he was very inconsistent, which to me has always been one of the signs of an athlete using drugs. But in Reynolds's case that inconsistency was the trademark of his career. I felt Butch was confused when running against me and others. He would change his strategy each time he competed, looking for a solution but in the process learning nothing and gaining no consistency. He was obviously talented and dangerous, so I knew that as long as I never let him beat me it would keep him guessing and experimenting, which would also keep him inconsistent.

Yes, I knew my competitors well. I never stopped studying them during my entire career, since every year it seemed that there was someone who was supposed to be the new whizz kid who was going to take over and beat me. As much as sprinting is about executing a good race strategy and executing it well to run a fast time, it is also about racing against your competitors, and the more you know about those competitors the better.

Being able to read the athletes I ran against boosted the confidence I'd gained from giving 100 per cent in every single training session. But I had to make sure that my knowledge about them didn't upset the delicate balance required for races. You want to know your competition as much as possible, but you must also remain focused on your own strategy as well and not allow what you know about your rivals to deplete your energy. Nor should you risk engendering negative energy by thinking about them come race time. So in those few minutes before the gun went off, no matter who was competing against me, I would see the other racers as all the same: seven people standing between my goal and me. Instead of thinking about them, I focused on what I needed to do.

RAZOR-SHARP FOCUS

The ability to focus was one of my most valuable traits when it came to becoming a successful Olympic athlete. That ability to compartmentalise my thoughts and focus on the task at hand was also aided by the fact that I'm naturally a very organised person who operates best when my work environment is clean, neat and uncluttered. I think someone who is much less organised and who is naturally a person who works better in a cluttered environment may not find it as easy to go into the deep focus that's required in these moments.

When under pressure during training or competition, great athletes are able to think only about execution. They can defend themselves against potential distraction and have developed the ability to recognise when they are becoming distracted and immediately make the necessary mental adjustment.

Inevitably, if you have the physicality, the talent and the work ethic, you find yourself going nose to nose with some of your heroes. That can be disconcerting, to say the least. Sally Gunnell remembers coming up against Shirley Strong, who she had watched win a silver medal in the 1984 Olympics. 'She was that role model, a glamorous sort of person, even though she smoked in those days! That probably wasn't the best thing, but she looked great and was a great hurdler. She was part of it. Then all the sudden we were both competing in the 100 hurdles championship race at the Commonwealth Games. I remember thinking, "My God, I've watched and admired this girl for the last four

years. And here I am next to her. What do I do?" That was
when I realised, "You know what, you've got to go do your
best."'

I had the same experience with Calvin Smith, who I
always thought was so great. Even though I was a 200- and
400-metre runner and he was the 100-metre world record
holder at one point, I emulated him to some degree when I
first started in the sport at the professional level. I remember
being in a race against him and thinking, 'Gosh, I'm so
lucky to even be able to line up against him.' Then I beat
him.

While some athletes are born with a superior ability to
focus, others are born with less capacity to concentrate or
compartmentalise their thoughts, so they have to train
themselves on that front. Either way, every athlete should
strive to be 100 per cent effective in his or her ability to
focus.

A lot of people don't really understand what it means to
focus. Being focused means to be totally in the moment and
totally about the task at hand and nothing else. So all one's
ability to execute is targeted on that task, which results in
the best possible chance of achieving success or performing
at one's absolute best.

I learned about the need for focus the hard way – and not
just once. In 1996 a lapse in focus led to my losing a pre-
Olympic race to Frankie Fredericks. He had been running
very, very fast early in the season, and had just missed
setting the world record in the 100 metres by one hundredth
of a second because he raised his hands in victory as he

crossed the finish line. Three days later in Oslo we both lined up for the 200 metres with Frankie in the lane just outside of me. My advantage over Frankie physically had been my ability to run the bend faster than him and put pressure on him by coming out of the bend ahead of him. Then I would use my 400-metre strength to hold him off. I knew that Frankie was in great shape and that I would have to really put a big gap between him and me coming out of the bend. I was still focused on that when the gun went off. So instead of reacting to the gun when it went off, I listened for it. As I would find out, the time it takes to react once you've heard the gun, as opposed to reacting to the sound of the gun, can be the difference between winning and losing. By the time I got out of the blocks, Frankie was gone, so I had to use a lot of speed early in the race to catch him. I came off the bend level with him, then used my strength to pull away from him down the home stretch. But I had used so much early in the race that I wasn't able to hold him off. With about five metres to go, Frankie pulled back even with me. I still could have won if I had thought to lean into the tape. Unfortunately, because I was usually ahead of my competitors, I didn't think to do that and lost the race to Frankie. But if I had been focused on what I should have been, it would never have been an issue.

Clearly, even the best of the best lose focus sometimes. As part of her quest to win the Barcelona Olympics, Sally Gunnell was determined to medal in the World Championships that preceded the Games. It looked like she would do that as she came off the eighth hurdle in the lead.

Instead of remaining focused, however, 'I'm thinking, how did I do that?' she said. Then she started worrying about all the people around her. 'I looked up at Sandra [Farmer-Patrick] and thought, "Oh God, she's up here too." I ended up losing focus, stuttering into the ninth hurdle, and having a ding-dong with Sandra over the tenth hurdle. Afterwards, I realised just what an important part the mind plays.'

As Sally recognised, all the training and ability in the world amounts to nothing if you aren't able to keep your mind exactly where it needs to be.

Rebecca Adlington also focuses on trying to execute from a technique standpoint and race strategy standpoint rather than on her competitors. That doesn't mean she disregards them. 'I know they're there. I know what times they did in the heats and how they're looking. I know the situation. I know roughly how they swim. I am very aware that this girl might come back strong, that girl is going to go out. I am aware of all that, but the most important part of my race is how I swim. I can't control anyone else. There's no point in worrying about them. I *can* control my own race. The most important thing is how I swim it.'

COMPETITIVE ATTITUDE

As we've seen, worrying about rivals creates focus problems. Ironically, so does fraternising with them. In 1992 I was number one in the world in the 200 metres and 400 metres and had been at that point for two years. At an early-season race in Rome before the Olympics in Barcelona,

I was again competing against Frankie Fredericks. At that point I was undefeated and had beaten Frankie, along with everyone else in the world, several times. In the call room just before the race I was sitting next to Frankie and we shared a laugh about something that had just happened. We were still laughing as we walked out on to the track. I got focused and got into my blocks. The gun went off and I executed my race as I normally do and crossed the finish line first. At least that's what I thought. So did the officials, who handed me the victory flowers and trophy. Halfway through my victory lap, my agent Brad Hunt yelled, 'I don't think you won.' I looked up at the stadium screen to see the race results and saw that indeed I had not won. Frankie had just out-leaned me at the very end of the race.

It was my first loss in over two years. I was in great shape and ready to run fast, but I had lost my edge to Frankie during that pre-race laugh. I would never make that mistake again. From that point on, there would be no talking, handshakes or pleasantries before the race. I refused to participate in any activity with my competitors. I just focused on my race strategy and treated each race as a battle, with every competitor seen as the enemy.

I didn't hate my competitors. I felt no disdain for them. But for me to be at my best I needed to be focused only on me. My new danger zone philosophy and method was tested a month later when I lined up for the final of the 200 metres at the US Olympic trials in New Orleans – it was my first real opportunity to make an Olympic team. I would be running in lane eight against the best in the world, including

Carl Lewis, Leroy Burrell, at the time one of the best 100-metre runners in the world, and Mike Marsh, who would go on to become the Olympic gold medallist at 200 metres that year. Since only three sprinters would make the team, I needed to be focused.

My refusal to pay attention to them in order to focus on myself paid off. I made the team. Many people, including my competitors, thought that my attitude or demeanour was meant to intimidate them, but it was not. It was first and foremost all about me and my focus on the task at hand and the race ahead.

I could gain an advantage over my competitors before ever stepping into the blocks simply by looking at them. While sitting in the call room with my head down, thinking only about my race, I would periodically glance up and catch one of my competitors looking at me. When I looked back at them, they always looked away. They would eventually look back at me, only to find me still staring at them. That scared them. Mission accomplished, race won.

Although I enjoyed making those athletes I didn't like squirm before a race, I regretted having to sacrifice my friendships with competitors like Frankie who I liked and respected. But that's just what I had to do to keep my race focus sharp. Winning was the priority.

Sebastian Coe and I talked about the inevitable fallout that accompanies the drive to win at all costs. 'If you get to the top level of your sport, there is a deep streak of selfishness,' he said. 'There has to be. There are friendships you can't accommodate during that period. My mother used to say that a week before a race I would barely recognise her even in the house! It's in your DNA. I was probably selfish enough to think I'm just not going to allow anything to intrude on something I've been doing for ten years and take very seriously.'

The recipe for success, however, isn't the same for all athletes, even those in the elite ranks. Since 2008, when the Jamaican Olympic track and field team took home a record number of medals in the sprints, many people have wondered, 'What is it about the Jamaicans that makes them so good?' Their great talent, of course, is a given. But the Jamaicans are also a very easy-going society. They don't worry about things as much, and tend to stress a lot less than those from many other cultures. Ironically, that slower pace and more easy-going approach to life have contributed to their championship performances of late, with Usain Bolt leading the way.

Prior to Usain, his Jamaican team-mate Asafa Powell was the fastest man in the world. But just like American Leroy Burrell, Asafa broke the 100-metre world record twice but never won a championship during that time. Interestingly, he was notorious for his very un-Jamaican demeanour at the championships, with the pressure he felt on the starting line clearly visible to competitors and spectators alike.

Usain, by contrast, exhibits a very relaxed and even playful demeanour on the starting line prior to his races. 'Yeah, definitely. I love to enjoy myself. I like to have fun. I'm kind of laid-back sometimes,' he told me when he arrived two and a half hours late for training at the University of West

Indies training facility. I was never late for training. 'A lot of people stand there focused, thinking about what they have to do. But for me, I know what I'm here to do, so all I've got to do is make sure I'm relaxed and I don't stress over the race too much.'

During the 2010 season, I happened to be talking to him in the warm-up area. As he joked and laughed, as he does often, I looked up to see that all of his competitors were walking out on to the track. His race was starting in less than ten minutes, yet his demeanour was the same as mine used to be after the race.

'I don't try to think about the race,' he explained. 'I think when you start thinking about everything in your mind at the start, "Gotta make sure this, gotta make sure that," all these little things start coming back and if you're not really focused, then you're going to throw off your race. That's what happens to a lot of guys out there. They're stressing so much they lose it.'

Of course, when you're as good as Usain you certainly don't have to worry as much as the other competitors. Neither did I. In order to be the absolute best I could be, however, I needed to be focused. That was my way. But other members of the Jamaican sprint team have followed Usain's way. Instead of going into a deep focus before the race and allowing themselves to feel the stress of the moment, they have found that they compete better when they take a more relaxed and easy-going approach to the race. And that is as natural to them as my deep focus is to me.

I was all business on the track, so I usually just focused on my own race. As always, I would visualise myself running my race, thinking only about my own performance and ignoring the rest of the field. My behaving as if they weren't even there – as if I was only running against the clock for myself – proved equally intimidating.

By the time I got into the call room, I knew I had done the work required and could beat them all. Would I? We would soon find out. My BBC colleague Colin Jackson often tells me he hated being in such close proximity with competitors with whom he would soon be walking out on to the track side by side, but I craved that pre-race moment. It's what I miss now that I'm retired.

PREPARING FOR BATTLE

Immediately before a race, great Olympic athletes are unaffected by potential outcomes, positive or negative. This is all about the heat of the battle, that time when you are in the most competitive environment. The competition is about to start in minutes and you know what you are capable of doing, you know what your competition is capable of doing, but you don't know if you will execute perfectly, horribly, or any of the many possibilities in between. You also don't know how each of your competitors will perform. They may have the performance of a lifetime today, they may perform just as you predicted and expected they would, or they may have a major setback today. The only thing that is certain is that the race will happen and there will be a result.

THE HEAT OF BATTLE

Great Olympic athletes are able at this time to detach their minds from everything else that is going on, so that they are only thinking about the competition – and only the things that will help them to succeed. This is where I think I was at my best. Of course I was nervous and anxious, and the automatic default mode for my brain at that moment was to think of the consequences of the result, since I was obviously conscious of the fact that, as much as I wanted to win and I believed wholeheartedly that I could win and would win, anything can happen. That's why we race – to see who will put it all together and take all of the different levels of talent, and different levels of work, and the different approaches to preparation, and execute best on that day in order to come out on top and take the gold medal.

I miss that nervous energy and anxiousness, when it feels like it's taking forever for them to let us race. At that point I can't wait for the gun to go off so I can race. But I also want to know. I want to know the result. Not just the result but *my* result. Did I do it? I know I thought I could, but did I? Even though going through those pre-race moments was very tough and I felt a tremendous (and uncomfortable) pressure at that moment, after it was over I wanted to do it again.

The athletes who can control their thoughts and focus, and think only about the competition, their own performance and what they need to do, win races. These days, however, I see athletes in the hour to two hours before their competition actually go over and check their phone to see if they have any phone calls or messages. I deliberately turned my phone off when I went to the track so that it wouldn't ring, and I certainly wouldn't check it, because there might be a message that could distract me and make me think of something else.

It's hard enough to focus and think only about the task at hand without inviting potential distractions. I always thought, there are few things that could happen that would cause me to decide not to run a race. And even if it was an emergency, there would be nothing I could do about that situation right then. So I always chose to turn my phone off and cut off all communication with everyone other than my support team in the couple of hours leading up to race time. This allowed me to focus only on the race and not risk any distractions from phone calls or messages. As for those distractions that I couldn't as readily control, I had developed a way to deal with that by reserving the time leading up to and during the competition to only think about the race. To do this I had to be very strict with myself and not allow any exceptions. This included even thinking about the outcome of the race, or what might or would happen immediately after the race, or even upon crossing the finish line.

Athletes will often start to think about the consequences of a loss or of victory before the race even starts, which is a major distraction.

They will also start to think about other competitors who are in such close proximity. It's hard not to start thinking about the athlete who has just crossed your path. And while you might start contemplating how you're going to race against them, that's not what you should be thinking about at that point, because you can't control what they will do.

THE HEAT OF BATTLE

Just before the race you want to be thinking only about those elements you can control and what is about to happen in a mere few minutes. Your mind, however, presents all of these distracting roadblocks, and you must have incredible discipline to prevent yourself, or your mind, from contemplating them.

RETAINING PERSPECTIVE

Of course, it helps if you don't let the sheer enormity of the Games and what's at stake overwhelm you. That's what initially happened to Jackie Joyner-Kersee. 'For me, the Olympics has been the foundation to me going on and having the other successes or successful years after that, because in 1984 I realised I had talked about going to the Olympics and I had dreamed about it, but I hadn't realised the magnitude of the whole Olympic movement,' she told me. 'I didn't really feel it until I was actually in the stands for the opening ceremonies – the anticipation from the fans and just the excitement when you sat there and watched each country come through.

'As I was sitting there, I became really anxious and nervous. I had set the Olympic record at the Olympic trials. Going into the Games, people had picked me to win the gold in the heptathlon, but I had strained my hamstring. I had never really been injured before and thought it was a pulled muscle.

'At the Games, I was focused on my leg so completely that I lost all the train of thought of how prepared I was to really execute to the best of my abilities – even with the leg being heavily bandaged. Each event, I went out there anticipating the pain, but I didn't really feel it. I didn't feel anything. After the high jump, the shot put and the 200 metres, my numbers were not so far off from what I had done at the trials. By the time we went down to the long jump on the second day, I was finally ready to go because the long jump is my favourite event. I committed two fouls and ended up far behind the board to just stay in the competition.'

Performing poorly on the long jump lost Jackie a lot of points. 'I was so bummed out I didn't even eat when [her coach] Bobby [who would later be her husband] told me to replenish my fuel. I sat off in the corner crying. Bobby pulled me over to the side with a very few, choice words. "The heptathlon is made up of seven events, and you've still got two events to go," he told me. By then I didn't care about my leg because I really wanted to win. I threw the javelin, and I remember lining up for the 800 metres. I ran the first lap, and then on the second lap on the back stretch Bob was telling me to pump my arms, but by then I had no more energy left. When I crossed the line I knew Glynis Nunn from Australia had won. I remember embracing her and congratulating her. She was like, "No, you won." I said, "No, you won." I knew.

'When I went into the press room and people said, "If you didn't have the injury ..." I let them know: "It had nothing to do with the injury. It was that I didn't perform." I had to accept that. I'll tell you, when I left Los Angeles I left there telling myself that if I was blessed to make another Olympic team I would be the toughest athlete out there mentally.'

I asked Jackie if she thought she had gotten caught up in the spectacle instead of being focused on the competition. She agreed that she had. The injury just accentuated her sense of being overwhelmed. 'Even though my physical therapist told me, "Jackie, you're ready," I didn't believe it because I wasn't accustomed to seeing my leg swollen,' she said. 'For whatever reason, the people who were the closest to me, I just disregarded what they were saying. I had a lot of doubt, because I just didn't think the leg was going to hold up.' Only when she looked at her times after the Games were over did she realise that her self-doubt had cost her the gold.

'At the 1984 Olympic Games I looked at myself in the mirror and I told myself – not to take anything away from Glynis Nunn – "The reason you didn't walk away from here as a gold medallist is because you didn't want it bad enough." When I left there, I trained and I told myself I wasn't going to let negativity get in the way of the success of my dreams. "I've got to think like a champion, and I've got to put myself in difficult positions and situations," I decided. "When my physical therapist or Bobby is telling me something, they are my eyes, they see the things I don't see, and I have to be on the same page with them."

'When I left Los Angeles, I said, "God willing, you give me another shot at this, no one, no one is going to beat me mentally. If they beat me, it won't be because of a mental breakdown. It will be because they were just better than I was on that day."

'That's why I fought through the asthma I was diagnosed with as a freshman in college. Even though I know it's a condition, I saw it as a sign of being weak and I couldn't let it get me. I started using asthma as an opponent. The asthma's like the Germans and the Russians, like they were trying to beat me. That was my mindset. There were times when I prayed and prayed that I would never have an attack in a competition. My biggest fear was going somewhere and not being able to do the 800. Or if the weather got bad or I had an allergic reaction. That weighed on me so much. I could train and do all this, but there were some days when I could run a mile on Monday, but Tuesday if there was fresh cut grass and all that, I would have a reaction to it. That's why I tried to stay on top of everything, to make sure that my immune system wouldn't break down. I couldn't afford to go on any medication or prednisone, because it would sap my muscle strength and make me unable to compete.'

Jackie's prayers for a second shot at the Olympics, asthma notwithstanding, were answered when she made the 1988 US team for the long jump and the heptathlon. She didn't go into the Games 100 per cent healthy. Her left knee had tendonitis on the patella. But that didn't matter. 'After what I had gone through in 1984, I remember telling myself, "I don't care; I am willing to pull every muscle in my body to get it done. I'm going to be positive. I'm going to get through this." I remember one of the reporters said, "You're behind.

You're not going to break the record. Where are you going to make the points up?" I wasn't even thinking about the points. I went up to this guy and said, "You know, I'll find a way. God will help me."'

Jackie had learned about running her own race the hard way the year before when she just barely missed her chance to break the world record because her opponents teamed up against her and went out slowly. 'I realised from that point on that I would not depend on anybody else to bring me to a pace, so I started learning my own pace.'

That lesson, coupled with what she had learned in the 1984 Games, would cement her career. She would go on to win three gold medals in the Olympics, four gold medals in the World Championships and one gold medal in the Pan American Games. She also became one of my heroes after I arrived on the Olympic scene. I watched her not only compete with confidence but handle her training sessions and preparation with the utmost professionalism.

UNLIKELY MOTIVATOR

Great athletes are able to understand themselves and how they naturally deal with pressure, but that doesn't mean that they naturally do it well or like it. I was a pressure performer, but that didn't mean that I enjoyed it. Pressure is uncomfortable to everyone and it was uncomfortable to me. But I found a way to deal with the pressure and not allow it to control me. Then I took it a step further and figured out how to take the pressure and turn it into a motivator.

So although I never loved the feeling of being under pressure, I loved how I made it work for me.

As a result, I was immune to the pressure that kills some athletes' careers. As an elite athlete, however, pressure doesn't just exist during competitions. The better you get, the more you have to not only compete in the limelight, but live in it too. And that came with its own set of challenges which I, for one, found especially hard to deal with.

8.

LIVING AND COMPETING IN THE LIMELIGHT

When I was competing, absolute 100 per cent focus was necessary for me to perform at my best, and the only way I could be sure of achieving that 100 per cent focus was to have 100 per cent control of my environment. So you may wonder why I decided to let NBC cameras follow me during my bid to win double gold at the 1996 Olympics. In the moment when I need to be focused the most, I would have a camera in my face every time I turned around.

Why had I agreed to that?

A few months earlier, I was going to be photographed for the *Sports Illustrated* Olympic issue and would most likely be featured on the cover. I had already been photographed for the cover of *Time* magazine's Olympic issue. The day the photographer came to photograph me for *Sports Illustrated*, however, I was training alone in Dallas, away from Coach.

My training sessions were always conducted with the same seriousness and focus as for a competition and I didn't like distractions. If someone tried to talk to me during my training session I got offended. 'How would you appreciate it if I came on to your job and started taking pictures of you and asking you for an autograph while you were at your desk trying to get an important report out?' I might even ask the intruder.

I could be a real ass, even if there was some justification. But I was not particularly understanding in those days, a less than stellar trait which re-emerged the day the *Sports Illustrated* photographer showed up. I wasn't in a very good mood anyway and just wanted to get my training session done without the cameras around. But the photographer kept asking me to do more and more takes so that he could get the shot he wanted. I finally snapped. 'I'm a professional and good at what I do,' I barked. 'You're a professional and good at what you do. So you should be able to get the damned shot without me having to run a million times.' We finished the shoot despite a definite sense of tension, and *Sports Illustrated* put the USA women's basketball team on the cover.

This was my chance to redeem myself with the media. NBC had sent a producer and camera crew down to get some footage of me training for one of the profiles they would show about me during the television coverage of the Games. But I had a rule that I didn't allow anyone to film my practices. Just as I sought perfection in every race, I looked for perfection in practice. Since that ended whenever onlookers were present, I wound up keeping my practices closed. I just couldn't afford the disruptions.

So we compromised. The film crew could be there, but would have to stay behind the fence that went around the track since I certainly wouldn't feel comfortable with cameras two feet from my face while I was trying to work. Even though those television cameras have huge lenses that can zoom in, the camera guys and producers hated being kept at a distance and would keep trying me. Finally they tried one too many times. I was never a person to go off and scream or yell at people, but I answered with a firm, deep-voiced 'No' accompanied by a glaring and effective stare.

A couple of weeks later, my agent Brad finally confronted me. I would need to lighten up on some of my rules and be a little bit more accommodating to the media if I wanted to capitalise on the Olympic opportunity from a marketing standpoint.

Apparently the shoot's producer had come back saying that I was extremely difficult to work with and they had gotten nothing that really told much of a story. 'They are planning to focus on you as the primary story of these Games, but they want access,' Brad told me, adding that they wanted to follow me each day. I saw the look on Brad's face and I knew he was right. The smart thing was to agree. So I did.

It turned out that having the cameras follow me over the Opening Ceremonies weekend wasn't so bad. I actually had a good time with the camera guys, joking and being myself.

They were very pleased with what they got and couldn't believe how much access I gave them and how much I seemed to enjoy it. But I hadn't been about to race then. All that would change in three days' time, when I would be competing in one of the biggest races of my life. Truth be told, I was a little afraid and would need to be more focused than I ever had been before.

Still, I knew I was in the best shape of my life. I had just had the most incredible training session of my career.

'Shouldn't you be able to deal with some cameras?' I asked myself.

'Yes, you should,' I answered. 'But do you want to take that chance?'

I did not. I wanted to retain absolute control, so that I could retain absolute focus. So I proposed a compromise. There could be no talking to me and I would not be talking to the camera crew. They could have a camera with me, but they had to stay a few feet away. They were happy with the compromise. As it was, it would take even more focus from me to block out the cameras and concentrate on what I needed to do.

In hindsight, I wish I had interacted better with the media as an athlete. But I felt insulted when interviewers asked me questions that they felt would generate the answers they were fishing for. It was like they felt they were smarter than me. I didn't like that. Being competitive, I set out to show them that I was actually as smart as them or smarter. That would cause some tension between me and some of the media, but it didn't impact on the work I did on the track.

LIVING AND COMPETING IN THE LIMELIGHT

COPING WITH FAME

I'm far from being the only champion athlete who has struggled with the seeming omnipresence of media and public attention. Athletic stardom certainly brings ample financial rewards. Athletes, at least those in mainstream Olympic sports, who previously struggled to make a living become financially comfortable if not downright wealthy. But that comes at a personal cost that's higher than most people realise. Cathy Freeman admitted to me that being thrust into superstardom after her Olympic home victory probably cost her a longer career. 'I wasn't comfortable with it then and I still am uncomfortable with it today at times. I still have a hard time coping with the glare and the attention of that night. People still come up to me and they're still blown away, telling me their story and their memory of that night. Part of me wants to disengage. I want to move on now. For me, it was such a business trans-action, in a sense. I know you get this. You get on with it, get it over and done with, and get out of there. The whole political case, arguments came into it. There's no more energy for emotional engagement, because it's hard work. It's hard to take on that beautiful burden and responsibility into your future, because then the precedence has changed. I didn't mean to become an agent of change ever in my whole life. I was just a girl trying to be the best runner I could be.'

To avoid her sudden stardom at home, Cathy didn't compete the year after the Olympics, choosing to leave Australia as often as possible. 'In hindsight, and hindsight's a great time, I really believe that my running career had ended as soon as I crossed the line in Sydney,' she told me. 'I found it really hard to find that same level of discipline and application that only comes from when you really want to do something. I was taking shortcuts in my workouts. I just felt like a bit of a shadow next to the athlete I used to be, next to the woman I used to be.'

As Cathy's story reveals, public scrutiny is one of the most difficult issues to contend with. That's certainly been the case for Usain Bolt, who has suddenly found himself in the middle of a media storm, with unceasing demands on his time. 'It's always so much,' he says. 'Every day people want me to do this, do that. It's hard for me because I just want to be a normal guy, play some PlayStation, play some football, chill with my friends.'

The demands are particularly hard for someone like Usain who is a homebody at heart. When I mention that one of the advantages of being in an international sport like athletics is getting to travel all around the world, make international friends and experience other cultures, he says that while he likes being on the road he doesn't go out. 'A lot of people like to see sights. I'm not like that. I'd rather stay in and watch TV, play on my video games, listen to my iPod, or whatever. That's how I am.' Most telling, perhaps, is the destination that caught his fancy. 'I really enjoyed Monaco,' he told me. 'I was wondering if I could get a place there. As I said to the Prince, "It's quiet." The people who are there are like I am, so you won't get bothered that much.'

Usain is clearly still wrapping his head about his new-found fame and fortune, along with the burden of single-handedly carrying athletics and the continued suspicions that come with obliterating world records.

People assume when you become famous that you sought and continue to court that celebrity. While that's true for many athletes, a few of us just wanted to go fast or do our sports to the best of our abilities. Suddenly, because of your accomplishment, you become public property.

That's what happened to me in 1996. By the time that incredible year was over, so many things had changed in my life. I started the year as a world champion sprinter and one of the best athletes in my sport. In my sport I was known and I was doing quite well financially from my endorsement deals with Nike and Ray-Ban sunglasses. But I wasn't famous. Track is a small sport relative to the entire world of sport, which includes team sports and those like tennis and golf that benefit from the fact that they are also recreational sports. That attracts a lot more fans, and thus sponsorship, advertising, television revenue and of course visibility. Ironically, I was better known in the UK and around Europe where I competed than I was in the US. That wasn't a problem for me since I enjoyed my anonymity. I was happy and enjoying my life as a single man and my new success.

By the end of 1996 I was a double Olympic champion and world record holder and the undisputed king of my sport. I had accumulated a larger portfolio of endorsement agreements than any previous US Olympic athlete. I had a book coming out, my own personal Swatch watch, and I was being paid more money to make appearances than I was to compete. I had become a wealthy individual. I was dating the supermodel Tyra Banks. I was no longer bigger in Europe than I was in the US. I couldn't go anywhere without people asking for autographs or pictures or just wanting to talk to me.

That took some getting used to. I wasn't used to not being in control. I wasn't used to having to deal with so many fans and requests for my time. I wasn't used to having to interrupt whatever I might be doing to accommodate a fan request. Before long, I realised how much I disliked that side of what my success had engendered. I started to stay home more. I became less trusting of strangers. I started to be more aware of my surroundings at all times, and I am still that way now. From the time I achieved my goals in Atlanta at the 1996 Olympic Games until this point, and I'm sure for the remainder of my life, I must be careful about what I don't do, what I do and how I do it. I have to adjust how I live my life because I've become a celebrity.

You have to learn how to deal with life in the limelight. Just like the way strangers feel entitled to pat a pregnant woman's belly, a boundary gets erased. It doesn't matter if you're having a quiet dinner out with your family. If you don't disrupt that to give someone an autograph, you're in the wrong. I actually got an email once from a guy who said what a shame it was that he had helped me get to where I was by contributing money to the Olympic Committee, and then I didn't give him an autograph at a restaurant.

LIVING AND COMPETING IN THE LIMELIGHT

While many athletes do court celebrity, some of us just want to go about our lives. That's not always easy. Nine times out of ten, the person who comes up to me expects me to drop what I'm doing and leave the people that I'm out having a good time with or my family. I'm supposed to ignore the people I'm with and basically tell them, 'You come second to my fans. My fans are first.' Because that's what that fan is used to getting. Most other athletes will do that. They don't want to annoy any fan, because that's where their stardom comes from, and they've got to make sure they keep feeding that stardom.

That's just not me. Although since 1996 I have been defined – and will continue to be defined – as the Olympic champion who made history in the Atlanta Games, I'm the same person now that I was before. I don't think that the success, the celebrity, the realisation of a dream or any of that changed me for good or bad. I had always tried to be the best person I could be and I was already confident in myself on and off the track. But for the first time after '96 I started to seriously consider the next phase of my life. I started to contemplate starting a family and what type of career or interests I would pursue after my career ended. And I started to think about when and how my career would end.

Clearly my life had changed. From 1990 when I first started my professional career as a sprinter until I retired, the timeline of my life was based on the four-year cycle of the Olympic Games. Prior to 1996 I was in a mode in which I was very much trying to reach my potential and establish myself as the best ever in my sport. I was the ultimate competitor at that point. Between Atlanta and Sydney I was in a mode where I was trying to break through limits and set new standards, not just on the track but as a sprinter who was doing things unprecedented in the sport on the track and off the track. I had transcended track. People knew me not just as a great sprinter but as a celebrity. After Sydney my life has been all about taking the platform that was established as a result of Barcelona, Atlanta and Sydney and building businesses that provide services and products to help other people achieve success based on the philosophy that I established over my career. In other words, I have managed to use the celebrity that my running engendered to strive for and achieve new goals in new arenas. But the goal is not – and has never been – fame.

I never expected the kind of renown that, for better and for a little worse, would define my life. That's not the kind of neighbourhood I came from. The same holds true for Rebecca Adlington.

'Getting into swimming, you never think, right, I'm going to be on TV or famous, because it's such a small sport,' she told me when I asked her about dealing with the celebrity that has accompanied her success. 'Before Beijing it was absolutely fine. You just went about your day as it was. After Beijing I suddenly got major commitments and all that sort of stuff that goes along with winning gold medals. It was really different and I struggled at the start because I didn't have the balance away from the pool. As soon as I was away from the pool, I was talking about swimming.'

LIVING AND COMPETING IN THE LIMELIGHT

Before her success, Rebecca had left her work in the pool, much like the way most of us leave our work at the office. When she suddenly found she was famous, 'it affected me', she admitted. 'I felt the pressure and I couldn't get away from it. I couldn't find something to just relax.'

That proved overwhelming. 'I didn't have an agent in Beijing. You just don't if you're a swimmer. When I came back, all this stuff was thrown at me. It was a rush to find an agent to deal with that. I managed to get an amazing one, and learned what I am comfortable with and what I'm not. But I still don't like the attention. I'm just not that sort of person. I think some people desperately want to be famous and be on TV. Not me.'

LIVING IN THE PUBLIC GLARE

Rebecca still seems uncomfortable with her sudden fame, especially in her home town. 'Nobody where I grew up was ever famous. I'm the only celebrity, if you want to call it that, from Mansfield. It's such a small place, there's no one else.' She's even more uncomfortable with living under the microscope – or through the looking glass. Like Alice, she feels like she's stumbled down a rabbit hole and into a world she wasn't brought up in and doesn't quite understand. Foremost among those elements that bewilder her is the criticism levelled at her by the press and public alike. All too often, the barbed – and even nasty – comments focus on her appearance.

She confessed to me how difficult it is to have people judge her outside the pool. 'I know I'm not the most attractive girl in the world. It doesn't bother me. It's one of those things. I'm not trying to be a model. I'm not in the papers because I want to be pretty. I'm just a swimmer!'

Physical appearance has never been a problem for Rebecca because she loves swimming. Indeed, the body that is judged harshly on land is part of what has earned her gold. That makes the constant criticism all the more baffling. 'I don't understand why people have to comment on how I look and think they can have a go at me for it. People will email or text, "God, you're ugly." Why would you say that to someone? I would never send that kind of message to anyone, whether I knew them or not. What goes through people's heads to say that sort of thing? It's unnecessary and hurtful, but they just don't care.'

'Back off,' Rebecca would love to tell her critics in both the public and private forums. 'I just want to swim.' Instead, she does her best to simply ignore it. 'It's got to the point where I don't read the paper. I don't look online. My dad gets all those Google Alerts or whatever. I won't do any of that for myself. I will not Google my name. I don't like looking at the criticism. I don't see the point of putting that in my head and making me feel insecure about something that is not what I'm trying to do. As a woman especially, when you're getting knocked all the time it's very difficult to be confident. And I'm a confidence swimmer. I need to feel confident before a race. So if somebody sends me a message or something on Twitter or Facebook, I delete it straight away. Even though I know that I'm extremely good at my sport, I don't want some comment about something I can't control to affect the confidence I have in the pool.'

Being the public butt of jokes by people like comedian Frankie Boyle, who made some unpleasant comments about her appearance on the BBC's *Mock the Week* in August 2009, created a fallout that proved even more hurtful.

Rebecca claimed that the jokes didn't hurt her feelings. 'I love comedians,' she told me. 'I am the first person to take the piss out of myself. I am the first person to laugh at things like that.' However, when Boyle was publicly chastised because of the flood of complaints triggered by his bad taste, people blamed Rebecca. 'Everyone was so hurtful about it,' she said. 'They attacked me, saying that I was the reason that he got thrown off, that I should just get over it or have plastic surgery. I couldn't actually believe these people. I didn't do anything. I haven't even spoken about it in interviews. I didn't even care about the comments.'

The level of very personal, undeserved criticism that Rebecca has had to deal with is hard to fathom, let alone understand. But most successful athletes, especially Olympic champions, become the focus of public attention and wind up living in the limelight. Nadia Comaneci would prove a notable exception. Not that she wasn't the media darling in 1976. She was voted the 1976 BBC Sports Personality of the Year in the overseas athletes category and named as the 1976 'Female Athlete of the Year' by both UPI and Associated Press, but her accomplishments weren't heralded the same way back home in Romania. Although she was named a 'Hero of Socialist Labour' she wasn't a huge celebrity in her own country, in part because television programmes only aired there between 7 p.m. and 11 p.m. at that time. 'Media was not allowed to come into the country and interview me,' she recalled. 'Everything was controlled by the government, so I wasn't bothered by any kind of media at all. The only thing that was a big surprise after I won the Olympics were the crowds of people who would come to see me compete. "I wonder why they do that?" I thought.'

The lack of fanfare shielded Nadia Comaneci from the pressures of celebrity. However, her sudden popularity brought with it the inevitable pressure to perform up to a new level of expectation. Nadia, who would receive the Olympic Order, the highest award bestowed by the International Olympic Committee, in 1984 and 2004, suddenly felt that she had to be even better than before. I asked her if that made competitions more difficult. 'No, it just makes you more nervous when you compete,' she said. 'But once the music starts, and you go on an event, that kind of goes away a little bit. I was very well prepared at all times. I knew I was very well prepared. But at the same time I knew I could make a mistake, because it takes very little to mess it up. And I've done it a couple of times.'

For those athletes not protected from the limelight like Nadia, Sally Gunnell may just have the answer. Towards the end of her career Sally felt the pressure of media scrutiny even more than she had at first. 'I went through a stage where I was almost trying to be somebody else, because you think you should,' she said. 'I've learned just to be yourself. That probably goes back to that self-doubt that I've had to fight through the years, but it's something I pass on and take with me now. You know what? Someone doesn't like you? That's their problem. This is me. Be yourself. Just get on with it.'

That's not a lesson that Daley Thompson ever needed to learn.

'What's the one personality trait that you feel contributed most to your success as an athlete?' I asked him.

'What are my options?' he asked.

'Well, there's your confidence,' I answered. I think the supreme confidence that allows Daley to blaze his own path without worrying about what others think gave him an unparalleled edge. Even now, for example, he will show up to evening functions, no matter how formal, in the shorts, T-shirt or polo shirt and trainers he's always worn. The closest he gets to a suit and tie is a jogging suit. That's what he's always worn all of his life and that's what he continues to wear, even if the rest of us are in tuxedos.

Being his own person and saying whatever is on his mind without a second thought has led to some significant run-ins with the media. 'I think it was more an issue for them than it was for me,' Daley told me. 'The media summon you to the press room as if they're royalty. And then they just want to tear you down. I was never in it for attention or celebrity. I just wanted to be good at sport and didn't need either of those. So I had no need for the media. And the media have a problem with people who don't need them.'

MEDIA MANAGEMENT

Ironically, like Muhammad Ali, Daley managed to control the media because he said what he wanted to say, wasn't political about it, and didn't care about the consequences of what he said. He had his points and he was going to make them. Years after his athletic career, Muhammad Ali ultimately became a hero to more people than ever worldwide. As Daley gets farther away from his competitive years he seems to have mellowed somewhat and the public seem to have embraced him more. But along the way I am sure there have been some missed opportunities, because being politically correct has traditionally been something of a prerequisite for endorsements and appearances for Olympic athletes. But I'm also sure that, even knowing this in hindsight, Daley would still rather be himself than compromise who he really is in exchange for any financial opportunity.

But it's not just about how others – whether the public or the media – react to you once you achieve the fame that so often accompanies athletic success at this elite level. It's how you, the athlete, deal with it.

Getting caught up in the whole celebrity thing is a huge danger for athletes, especially once they achieve Olympic stardom. Prior to 1996 I was much better known outside the US, where track was a much bigger sport, than I was inside the US, where track can't compete with the big team sports. But as a result of my performance in Atlanta in 1996 I was offered opportunities to become spokesperson for – or investor in – companies. I was offered television and movie parts. I was invited to all kinds of celebrity parties and events across the US. I wasn't interested. I was always thinking, 'I've got a season starting next year. Even though it sounds kind of fun, I can't do all this stuff. I have to get ready to run again.'

I am sure I left many opportunities on the table when I was at the height of my celebrity after the 1996 Olympics. At the time I didn't see this as a sacrifice, because I was so focused on training and maintaining my athletic dominance. I saw myself first and foremost as a track athlete, and I always put that first even after I got famous. My life was really designed to revolve around my track career. It was my job, my hobby and my favourite pastime. So other things just didn't fit.

These days, however, too many athletes focus on cementing their celebrity instead of their careers. In this reality television era there's a huge desire to get their face and name out there. In the past the only opportunity to embrace your fame and get out there as much as possible was when you were at competitions and there was media around to report on you. Now these athletes can be much more pro-active in developing the celebrity status that comes with having had Olympic success. So they have websites and Facebook and MySpace pages. Last year, while covering the European Championships for the BBC, I noticed that British 400-metre runner Martyn Rooney tweeted something after his quarter-final. When I ran into him I said, 'Martyn, stop tweeting and just focus on running.'

At the end of the day, it takes a lot of focus to be an Olympic athlete. As soon as you come off the track from a race, your focus has to be on your performance. How did that go? How did I run? Let me sit down and catch up with my coach as quickly as possible so we can review it and figure out what adjustments we need to make in the semi-final. If your focus is on having more Twitter followers than someone else and getting to your phone and tweeting about how the race went, you're competing in the wrong arena and for the wrong reasons. You're no longer interested in being a great athlete. You just want to be famous.

There is a skew in terms of values right now that is soci-etal. There are a lot of people who are really well known for doing absolutely nothing or for doing the wrong thing. We also live in a very litigious society, where we want to essen-tially do anything except take responsibility for our own actions. All of these general societal issues that we're deal-ing with, including the sense of entitlement that the younger generation seems to have developed, is reflected in the microcosm of the athletic arena. So instead of concentrating on finding ways to improve their performance, it's often about image instead.

Of course, it can be argued that I was too focused on my athletic career and that I should have been more accessible while I competed. The fact is that dealing with the media would remain a challenge during my entire racing career. Even at the beginning, when the coverage was all pretty positive, I found it overwhelming and somewhat uncomfortable. The fact that the coverage eventually started to turn negative made everything that much worse.

TARGETED

The portrayal of the 150-metre Fastest Man in the World challenge against Donovan Bailey was a shock to me. After the Olympics in 1996, when I ran 19.32 seconds to win the gold medal at 200 metres in Atlanta, people began to call me the fastest man in the world. Traditionally that title has always automatically gone to the current 100-metre world record holder, world champion or Olympic gold medallist. In 1996 all three of those titles belonged to Donovan Bailey. Donovan had broken the world record for 100 metres at the 1996 Olympics and in that same race he won the Olympic gold medal. On top of that, he was already the defending 1995 world champion. Yet because I had run faster over 200 metres in terms of miles per hour than anyone else previously in history, there was an argument that I was the fastest man in the world.

Being labelled the fastest man in the world didn't really matter to me because that's never been an official title. What mattered most to me was that I was the Olympic gold medallist at 200 metres and 400 metres, and that I had accomplished what no one else ever had. I was proud that I had run the 200 metres so fast that people were starting to rethink the unofficial fastest man title. But it didn't go beyond that.

Donovan, however, I think felt slighted once people started calling me the fastest man in the world. And even though he and I had had a good relationship of mutual respect, I felt he started to treat me differently. Then the media started to talk about a match race between Donovan and me to determine who really was the fastest man in the world.

I never backed down from a challenge. I sure wasn't about to shy away from this one, especially since in trying to persuade people that *he* was the fastest man in the world, he chose to talk negatively about my accomplishments to the media. There was no way I was going to tolerate that.

I had noticed that Donovan had not had a very good season going into the 1996 Olympics as the defending world champion. He had had many sub-standard races, had not won very many races on the European circuit, and did not look impressive in the early rounds in Atlanta. Even in the final of the 100 metres, for the first half of the race he wasn't winning, although he did pull out the victory in stunning fashion and broke the world record to win the Olympic gold. I pointed out to the media how inconsistently he had run lately, adding that I had respect for how he was able to pull out a victory when the pressure was on. 'But if I line up against him for 150 metres,' I concluded, 'there is no way he will beat me.'

The press only reported my comments about Donovan's inconsistency at the beginning of the season and my claim that he would never beat me. That started an even bigger firestorm and rivalry. So promoters started to talk with my agent and Donovan's agent about a race between us over 150 metres. There was a lot of buzz about this race and a lot of excitement about the potential showdown between the two of us. I felt that there were other people who legitimately had a claim to this title of fastest man in the world and that they should be allowed to be part of the race as well. A field including world-class runners like Linford Christie, representing Great Britain, Ato Boldon, who had won a bronze at 100 metres as well as 200 metres in Atlanta, representing the Caribbean, Frankie Fredericks, who had just won silver at 100 metres and 200 metres, representing Africa, and American Carl Lewis, one of the biggest names in the sport at the time, would have been an incredible and truly global race of the fastest men in the world. Donovan disagreed.

Ultimately it was decided that a head-to-head showdown between Donovan and me with no other athletes would be best. I agreed because I just wanted to race. The event was scheduled for May 1997 in Toronto. In the months leading up to the race, however, Donovan seemed to be unable to talk about his own chances of winning the showdown race without trying to discredit my abilities. The media ate it up. And although I didn't want to respond, preferring to talk about my own accomplishments and why I could win the race, I couldn't let his taunts go unchallenged.

Still, I focused on my training and arrived in Toronto ready to run. From the moment I got there I was caught off guard, which I hate. Unbeknownst to me, this had become an American versus Canadian affair, with everyone on Donovan's home turf hoping that he would beat me. The Canadians, who have always had a bit of an inferiority complex being so close to the US, were beside themselves with the fact that in Donovan Bailey they had an Olympic sprint champion who was better than the neighbouring Americans. He had also helped them overcome the embarrassment caused eight years earlier by Ben Johnson and his positive test and ban for steroids during the 1988 Seoul Olympics.

The race had been set up over 150 metres, with 75 metres on a curve and 75 metres on a straight. That was a race that I knew I could win. Donovan was not a great curve runner and I always have been. The fact that I was stronger than him also worked in my favour. After some last-minute nonsense on Donovan's part, including him saying in a press conference that I didn't really want to run against him, I decided to show just how confident I was in my ability to win this race by putting my money where my mouth was. Donovan and I had each been given $1 million to run this race, with an additional $1.5 million going to the winner. I now challenged him: 'I am willing, if you are, to put my $1 million into the prize money and winner takes all.' Donovan declined the offer.

Race day finally arrived. The gun went off and I got a great start. Then, abruptly, I pulled my quadriceps muscle, thereby ending the race. On crossing the finish line Donovan immediately started telling the media that I was faking the injury and that I didn't want to run against him. Of course the Canadian media fans supported him on this, which upset me. But I thought that I would be able to count on support from my own country. I was wrong. The criticism I received from the US media was as hurtful as it was disappointing. But that's America and that's what makes it different. It's a tough place that breeds tough competitors and tough athletes. American sports media don't support an athlete simply because he's American. They will criticise you just as much as anyone else. I was a big star, so I was a target.

PROVING MYSELF

After that race and during the remainder of the 1997 season I was determined to prove to the world number one that I wasn't a quitter or a faker and that I was the same fierce competitor that I had been when I went to the Olympic Games, the biggest event in athletics, and attempted do something that had never been done before. So when the doctor told me that I should not compete any more that season to let the injury heal, that was not an option for me. I continued to rehab and continued to train and eventually over-reached.

In my eagerness to get back out there and prove myself to the world, I went to Paris to run the 400 metres, a race that I had not lost in seven years. My fourth place finish clearly showed that I hadn't recovered from my injury. But a few media outlets talked about how this loss, coupled with what they called my 'loss' to Donovan Bailey in the match-up race, was evidence of post-Olympic complacency.

I was advised again by my doctor and my coach not to compete. But because I hadn't been healthy during the US championship and hadn't made the US team, the IAAF had actually instituted a new rule specifically to allow all defending champions an automatic entry to the 1997 World Championships in Athens. So I continued to train and showed up at the World Championships for the 400 metres far less than 100 per cent fit. In the first round I could feel that I wasn't 100 per cent. In the quarter-finals, feeling that I needed to conserve as much as possible I made a mistake and did not look around at the end of the race to ensure I had enough lead to win the heat, and I was passed by two competitors at the finish. I ended up not finishing as an automatic qualifier to the semi-finals, so I had to wait to qualify on a time basis. This caused people to cast further doubt and criticise. Their comments, however, didn't compare to those I levelled at myself. I remember silently sitting and waiting with my coach to find out if I had qualified for the semi-final, choking on my disappointment in myself.

Once the results came up and I had made it to the semi-final, I still said nothing to anyone, not even to the media. I couldn't wait for that semi-final. In that race I put it all together and ran faster than the personal best times of any of the competitors in the entire World Championship field. And I wasn't even healthy. Tyree Washington, one of my US competitors who was a new and up-and-coming athlete, had made some comments after my quarter-final that he didn't think I had the competitiveness or the drive any more and that it was over for me. When asked about that comment, I just said, 'I have nothing to say, only a race to run. I'm happy that Tyree has made the final so that he can be in it when I win it!'

When the final started, I felt confident that I could win, even though I knew it would be tough because I wasn't 100 per cent healthy or 100 per cent fit. When the gun went off, I tried to balance my race between careful execution and being competitive. At 200 metres I was in very good shape, but at 200 metres you start to make a move and start to run a little bit more aggressively. That's when I began to feel the injury and the soreness began to creep up in my quadriceps. I kept running regardless. At about 270 metres into the race, the inside of my leg near my groin felt as if I had pulled a muscle. Just as I was starting to slow down because I thought the race was over for me, I felt the pain release and let go. So I started running again. No longer in contention for first place, I was back in the second half of the field by this point. With 120 metres to go, I was probably in about sixth place. If there was ever a time to quit this was it. But I never even thought about quitting; it was not an option. The only thing I thought – and it was instinctive – was, 'I'm not injured. I can still run, so run.' And run I did. I put myself back into the race, passed the other athletes and ran away from them, finishing first and winning the gold medal.

To this day, that is one of the races I am most proud of, because of the competitiveness I showed and because I proved to the world that I was still the competitor that I had shown myself to be over the preceding six years. Even after that, I still wasn't given the benefit of the doubt. For example, in 1998, when I pulled out of the 200 metres at the US championships because of an injury, the media hypothesised that I was ducking Maurice Greene – who not only hadn't ever beaten me in the 200 metres, but who had never run anything close to what I had run. It was crazy.

At the same time, I was also criticised for not being friendly enough, funny enough or dynamic enough. This all came at a time when track athletes had started to call themselves entertainers. Long before Usain Bolt started clowning around, it had become common for the sprinters, especially in the 100 metres, to 'put on a show' as they called it at the start. Most of the sprinters saw their moment of opportunity to make themselves known or enhance their celebrity. So during the introductions before the race they would scream and yell, make funny faces, and do whatever other silly things they could to try to make the crowd laugh. Since many of the 100-metre sprinters are also 200-metre sprinters, some of this silliness found its way over to the 200 metres.

That wasn't something I was about to indulge in. Some of the athletes said that these antics helped them to relax before the race, but I didn't want to be relaxed at the starting line. Unlike many of my opponents, who I believe wanted to lessen the pressure of competition by pretending that this wasn't an important moment, I wanted to feel the pressure and run under the pressure of meeting the goals I had set for myself. Besides, the crowd had come to see a great race and to see me run fast.

By comparison to other sprinters, which the media didn't hold back on, I came across as stoic and too serious. But I didn't want to be an entertainer. I wanted to be a competitor and a winner. Somehow I was getting criticism for doing exactly what I was being paid record appearance fees to do.

The fact is that most people didn't really know me during those days, which is probably mostly my fault because I didn't let people see much of my personality. I was always a really private person, so I never allowed reporters and camera crews to get a look at the spontaneous everyday natural life of Michael.

MY MEDIA ICON

Muhammad Ali, one of my heroes, eventually provided me with a model when it came to dealing with the media. In 1995 I had taken a media-training course provided by one of my sponsors, during which we were shown some of his press conferences. The confidence he had and his ability to control the media were incredible to me. I wanted to be like him.

Up to that point I'd known Muhammad Ali just as one of the greatest boxers of all time. I had watched him fight on television a couple of times when I was kid, and my entire family and I rooted for him. The first time I ever felt sad about a sports event was when he lost one of those matches.

Despite those feelings, when I saw videos of Ali's press conferences in my media-training course, at first I just saw him as a trash talker. Then I started to get what he was doing. He not only controlled the media by just talking a lot, he showed incredible ability to make people laugh and ask questions about the topic he wanted to talk about. He was so funny, quick and witty. It was incredible to see.

I knew my personality wasn't even close to his and that I could never pull off interviews the brilliant way he did. So I developed my own ways of controlling the media that, ironically, I would later become a part of. I simply orchestrated events in which they could participate.

Of course, life in the limelight did have its perks. Becoming a celebrity has allowed me to be financially successful and live out some dreams. It has also provided the opportunity for me to influence the lives of many less fortunate people. I have supported a school in Oakland, California, for the last ten years, which provides a high-quality education to kids who come from a background of poverty and drugs, and really have no reason to be hopeful. Not only do I get the chance as a celebrity to talk to and influence these kids, but every year we have an auction to raise money for better facilities, teachers and supplies. I volunteer to appear at a cocktail party for the highest bidder and twenty of his friends or family. Last year I raised close to $100,000 for the school just by being a celebrity willing to spend time talking to people at a cocktail party!

I even got to meet the man who had helped me deal with the media. After watching Ali on that video I was mesmerised and wanted to know more. I started to read about him and discovered he was not only a great boxer, but a man who stood up for what he believed, stood up against authority when he believed authority was wrong, and was willing to sacrifice his career for what he believed. He became a Muslim, and although people thought he would change back, to this day he has not.

When I went to the Atlanta Olympics in 1996, I watched him light the torch at the Opening Ceremony. I was in the stadium and there had been great anticipation as to who would light the cauldron. Then Ali appeared and did the job, shaking the whole time from Parkinson's disease. It was an incredible thing to witness.

Later during the Games I attended a basketball game between the US and another country; at half time Muhammad Ali was presented with a gold medal from when he boxed in the Olympics in 1960. I was there for that as well. I watched the faces of the basketball players as they got a chance to meet him and I thought, 'That would be incredible.'

After I made history by winning gold in both the 200 and 400 metres, I was told by my agent, Brad Hunt, that Muhammad Ali wanted to meet me. I was floored! I thought Brad was kidding. The meeting was set up at the Atlanta hotel where Ali was staying, the Ritz Carlton. I was invited to his suite, where he greeted me with his wife and her sister. We talked for about five minutes and then he started telling me jokes. 'My wife's sister likes you,' he quipped.

We developed a friendship from there and I would see him at many other events. He wrote the foreword to my book, *Slaying the Dragon*, and he also came to my charity golf tournament to help raise money for kids with disabilities – he has always been generous with his time. He has the Muhammad Ali Parkinson Foundation, which supports Parkinson's research through an annual fundraiser. I attend that event any year that I can, and it is always good to see him. And while he has gotten progressively worse with the Parkinson's, he retains the wit he always displayed and continues to inspire me today. But then, I've been lucky when it comes to inspirations in my life and my career.

9.

COACHES, HEROES
AND MENTORS

'What do you want to be when you grow up?' my mother
asked me when I was about 12 years old. I told her that I
wished I could be one of the people I read about in the car
magazines I used to get from the library, who test-drove and
wrote about the fast sports cars. She sensed in my voice that
I didn't really believe I could ever be one of them. 'If that's
what you want to do, there's no reason you can't do that,'
she told me.

The sense of possibility she instilled in me was perfectly
balanced by my father's insistence on the need to have a
plan. Instead of telling me I could do anything I wanted,
from the time I was a young boy he always challenged me
about how I would accomplish things. One day he, too,
asked me about my plans for my future. I pulled out a
different dream and told him I was going to go to college to
be an architect.

'Do you know what it will take for you to graduate with a degree and pursue a career as an architect?'

I thought I had already answered the question by indicating that I was planning to go to college, so I didn't know what to say.

'You don't know, do you?' my dad insisted, his voice betraying his frustration. 'How do you expect to be successful with your goal if you don't know how you will achieve it?'

Of course, to achieve my dreams, whatever they might be, I knew I would have to work. As a kid, however, that wasn't exactly my priority. 'What's going on with you?' my mother asked me one morning as we headed to the bus stop that would take me to high school. Although I had been a pretty good student, at that period in high school my grades had dropped off. She didn't yell or get upset, but I could tell by her voice that she was disappointed in me. I thought about that for the rest of the day. Not wanting her to feel that way about me any more, I started to do better.

I was afraid of disappointing my mother, but I actively feared my father's wrath. The toughness that defined him had been instilled in him as a young child when his parents both went into the army, leaving him with his grandmother and aunt. They, aware that he was an only child and a boy being raised by two women, and not wanting him to be weak, treated him quite harshly. A stint in the military after high school further toughened him. As a very disciplined man with high moral standards, he has made few mistakes in his life. He expected as much from his children.

COACHES, HEROES AND MENTORS

That could be a burden. As a kid, I would walk home from school wondering if his car would be in the driveway when I rounded the corner. I knew that Mom would tell me to do my homework and chores, but Dad was sure to grill me about my assignments and how I did my chores.

Don't get me wrong. I love my father and I looked up to him. He was – and remains – my role model. I thought there wasn't anything he couldn't do. I wanted to be just like him. He was certainly not a wealthy man, but as a natural planner he was always in control. As an adult I see a lot of him in myself. And a lot of those characteristics helped me to achieve the success that I did.

PARENTAL SUPPORT

Parents played a major role in the success of many Olympic champions. 'My dad, who was a farmer, taught me the ethos of working hard,' said Sally Gunnell. 'You'd see him go out at five-thirty in the morning, and come back in late. Now looking back at it, that dedication to what you love – he loved what he did – and that focus and hard work was instilled in me from early on.'

Sebastian Coe's father wasn't just his inspiration. He became the double gold and double silver Olympian's coach. 'When I decided I wanted to get into track and field, I wasn't being prompted by my parents,' he told me. 'Even though my dad had raced competitively in cycling, his initial interest was purely paternal. He and my mum were a bit concerned about the fact that by the time I was 13 or 14, two nights a week and pretty much most of Sundays and half of Saturday afternoons, I was at somewhere called the athletics club. What was I doing? They wanted to make sure it was okay and that my life was balanced by other things like home-work. So my dad came down [to check things out].

'Having been on the fringes of a British cycling team in his youth, he understood the nature of endurance, along with the commitment required. For about a year he just sat around and listened and watched. Slowly, he came to the conclusion that what he was hearing didn't, in his world, make a lot of sense. Even though people kept saying, "Seb should be running eights in miles and running quick," every time I ran in a training session I seemed to be running slowly. Being the good engineer that he was, he started to ask some fairly basic questions, pulling apart what he saw and putting it together in a smarter way. Then, of course, he became completely obsessed with it.

'Over the space of the next five years or so, my old man gently guided me while slowly turning himself into a very proficient coach. He would actually often listen to footfalls with his eyes closed – just listening to the way your feet are coming down.

'Then he got smart. As a good engineer and good produc-tion engineer, he realised that you don't have to be the greatest physiologist in the world, but you do need to start bringing these people to the table, and effectively created a team. What was good was he was never afraid to be chal-lenged. If he set a training session and I asked, "Why would I be doing that?" he explained his reasoning.

'Having started out as a strategist and ended up as a deliverer, he then sat back on autopilot and watched it all happen. He always felt that good coaching involved building in self-obsolescence. His greatest pride came when for whatever reason we hadn't been able to speak for a few days.

'"What have you done in training?" he asked when I finally rang up. "That's fantastic," he said when I told him. "That's exactly what I would have asked you to do had I been there. I now begin to recognise that maybe 80 per cent of my job is done."

'Just before the 1984 Olympics, I got in to Los Angeles after training in Chicago. He had not seen me in three or four weeks, so when he came he said, "We'll go down to the track."

'It was about a week before, and I was doing four or five 400s at a fairly even pace – 50 seconds with tight recoveries of about a minute. After the third 400 he said, "I've seen enough. You're fine. Let's go have a burger."'

Seb's father had recognised that the necessary work had been done and no more was needed. He even used the same exact expression that my coach Clyde did. 'The hay is in the barn,' both men would say.

UNBEATABLE COACHES

Clyde, who would be my coach from 1986, when I finished high school, right through to 2000, when I retired, also shared Coach Coe's training philosophy. 'What do you think we're going to do today?' he would say at every daily practice. It was a test. If I got the answer wrong, he taught me why we weren't going to do what I had assumed and why we were going to do what he had planned. That helped me as an athlete, since I could execute the training a lot better when I knew exactly what we were doing.

To me Clyde, who is now in his late seventies, felt much more like a teacher than a coach. Even so, he accepted my input and even my challenges. If I asked, 'Why are we doing this? I'm thinking we should be doing something else,' he'd ask why. Sometimes my answers actually would make sense to him. In short, we had a partnership where we worked together.

Here, again, Sebastian Coe's relationship with his coach, who happened to be his dad, mimics my relationship with Clyde. 'He would structure stuff in a way that allowed you to fill in some of the bits,' Seb recalled. 'Looking back, however, the most important role he played in the first four or five years was stopping me doing things that I would have instinctively done that would have led to over-training and over-usage.'

Nadia Comaneci credits her coach with 50 per cent of her history-making gymnastic career. 'I always have said my success was possible because I was lucky to partner with my coach Béla,' she said. 'I think if he wasn't around, I wouldn't be able to deliver. When you're a kid of seven, eight years old, you have no direction where you should go, so you have somebody who is supposed to tell you what's good for you to do. He was a very good motivator. The best thing that he had which few others have was that he was able to prepare the gymnast to deliver the best at the most important time. If you're great in training, and two months later in the Olympic Games you aren't good, then who cares? You have to shine at the right moment. Orchestrating your climb involves an artistry that the coach needs to know how to do. You can't stay up for 12 months. If you have two or three competitions in a year, you have to go up and down, up and down. The coach definitely needs to calculate when you go down, so you can come up.'

To get the best from Nadia, Béla would drive her to improve her performance. 'This was great, but you can do better,' he would say. Even when Nadia earned a 10, he said, 'That was a great competition, but you can do better than this.' To fully tap her potential, he always pushed her to better and better performances by setting new goals and trying new moves. She likened that drive for improvement to my own. 'When you are the fastest at one Olympic Games, you're going to keep the time the same for the next Games? You have to be faster, no?'

The coach–athlete relationship is crucial to Olympic success. I often joke that Coach and I were a team, and when we won, we won together, but when we lost, it was his fault. The truth is that most of the time the wins can be attributed to the team but the losses are on the athlete.

There is a skill set required for coaching that many people aren't aware of. Often they assume that the biggest advantage a coach can have is the benefit of having played the sport they are coaching at the highest level. As a result, people tend to assume that I automatically went into coaching sprinters after my career, and they are surprised when I tell them that I am not coaching. Some will even tell me what a shame it is that I am not sharing my knowledge from my career with young sprinters. They don't realise that as a consultant to many sports organisations, as well as athletes and coaches not only in athletics but in all sports, I am sharing my knowledge from a career in which I learned plenty. But I know that I do not possess the skill set to be a coach. Coaching in a lot of ways is teaching, and that is why many of the best coaches have at one point taught school.

As the owner of Michael Johnson Performance my objective is to help athletes at all levels achieve their full athletic potential. In order to provide that level of support to those athletes, we not only need a wealth of sport training knowledge – to which I am a significant contributor – we also have to effectively communicate that knowledge to the athletes we train. We also have to be able to motivate them and get them to buy into what we are teaching them. It takes a certain personality and skill set to do that. After hiring over 20 different coaches for Michael Johnson Performance Centres, I have a good idea of the personality and skills that make a good coach.

Coaches must have the ability to motivate a variety of athletes, all of whom have different personalities and who respond differently to motivational techniques. When an athlete isn't giving his all, for example, or is not feeling particularly motivated about training, a coach has to understand that athlete as a person, as well as how to get the most out of that athlete and get him or her through the training session. Some athletes, for example, need an aggressive talking-to, so a coach will sometimes even go so far as to call those athletes out and question their toughness. This technique will cause some athletes to see themselves the way the coach is seeing them. When they don't like what they see and recognise that it is not the best attitude or approach to training, they will adjust. Another athlete may already not be feeling well or may be having a bad day. Being called out and talked down to by the coach just causes him to go further into his lack of motivation, to the point where he doesn't even want to be there at all. A good coach will get to know his athletes and understand how to read them.

Clyde knew me and knew exactly how to motivate me. He knew, for example, that for the most part I motivated myself. But he also knew me well enough to know when things weren't right. One day in 1999 during my pre-training stretch, a time when he and I would usually joke around or talk about things going on in the sport or just about anything else that didn't involve my training, he noticed that I was pretty quiet.

'What's on your mind?' he asked. I said nothing.

Even though the first part of the training session went okay, before we started the next part of the session he again asked me what the problem was. I told him I was not enjoying the sport any more because of all of the negative publicity I was getting, including being accused of ducking Maurice Greene and being criticised for not winning races by a large enough margin. Instead of lighting into me as I'm sure he wanted to, he knew how he needed to motivate me. I had always been focused on my own goals and cared little what was said or printed about me as long as I was winning and I was the best. So he reminded me first of the ridiculousness of anyone making the claim that I wasn't winning races by enough. He went on to remind me of our goal for the year which was to break the 400 world record and win a fourth consecutive world championship. Then he reminded me how my training over the last few months indicated that I was in the best shape I had been in since 1996 and that I was completely healthy for the first time since 1996. He ended by asking me the rhetorical question, 'Are you ready to start the second part of the training session?'

Of course I was. I felt a little stupid for feeling sorry for myself, and a little weak for allowing silly criticism, the kind of thing that I knew went along with being the best, to get to me and affect my training.

Good coaches like Béla and Clyde know how to get the best from their athletes no matter what the circumstances. They also know how to guide the athletes they work with, especially when they're young. When I met Clyde, my parents and I immediately knew that he was completely different from any other coach who had come to recruit me. At the time, although I had been offered scholarships at a lot of different schools, I was pretty much set on going to the University of Texas. Then Clyde, who would wind up coaching at Baylor for 42 years, came to my house. Instead of focusing exclusively on athletics, he talked a lot about the experience at the school and the quality of education I would get at Baylor. He talked about track and the experience of being part of the track team, but he talked equally about helping me develop as a young man. His objective was to teach young people, and he felt that track was a good way to learn lessons that would be helpful later on in life.

At the time, no one knew that I would go on to compete in the Olympics. I had shown the talent to be a good college athlete, but no more. My work with Clyde, once I committed to doing what I needed to do to get healthy, changed all that.

ATHLETE RESPONSIBILITY

Still, as much as I respected and listened to my coach, I retained command of the situation. Like the athletes I grew up watching and continued to look up to – people like Jackie Joyner-Kersee, Carl Lewis, Greg Foster and Sergei Bubka – I worked with my agent, manager and coach but accepted responsibility for my decisions and my actions, whether those involved competitions or contracts. But today many of the athletes, including some of those I work with, do not show this level of maturity. I don't see them as adult because they don't act like adults. And why would they?

Over the last ten years or so since athletes started to leave college early or to forgo it completely in favour of turning pro, the maturity level of the average athlete has gone down dramatically. Even though many of these athletes now compete in the professional arena, they still seek the team atmosphere that they had in college. They also still seek the guidance and control that some high school and most college coaches exert over their athletes. These young athletes simply aren't ready for and don't want the responsibility that comes with all the money and fame.

Coaches are also part of the problem. When I was competing not many athletes paid their coaches. Most athletes were coached even in their professional careers by their college coaches. When I first approached my coach about paying him, he refused and said that would only complicate things. I finally managed to convince Clyde that since he was helping me make a lot of money it was only fair that I should share and compensate him for his time and talent. Eventually coaches started to see how much money athletes were making and it became commonplace for athletes to pay for coaching services. As my coach predicted, that ultimately did complicate things. Coaches started to feel that they needed to justify their pay, so they started taking on larger roles with their athletes.

In the first half of my career my coach rarely travelled with me to meets in the summer and I was still able to achieve great success. Eventually, in the second half of my career he started to travel with me to most but certainly not all of my races. But I would have been successful whether he had travelled with me or not. Having him there with me was simply an added benefit.

Now, however, athletes feel that they can't compete without their coach at their side at every competition. Coaches, in turn, want to protect their meal ticket and make sure someone else doesn't steal their athlete. They also feel that they need to justify the fee they're being paid by being at every competition and making every decision for their charge, to the point where the athlete takes no personal responsibility at all for his or her own performance.

Even with this newly heightened role, coaching is sometimes a thankless job. While the coach–athlete relationship is a partnership and the coach is certainly partially responsible for the success of the athlete, it's the athlete who gets all of the glory. When coaches start to want more of the credit for their athletes' success and start to seek the glory by becoming what I call 'celebrity coaches', trouble is usually around the corner. Good coaches recognise that they are helping to guide the athletes. They know that, while their role is extremely important, they are not solely responsible for the athletes' success.

I have sometimes heard a coach say that an athlete would be nowhere without him. That may be true at some levels but not at the Olympic level. Olympic success is due to a number of things. Talent is certainly at the top of that list. Hard work, commitment and focus are absolute necessities. And the pressures of dealing with the expectations of your country, fans, family, friends, and your coach, as well as yourself, are carried by the athletes. As important as the best coaches are, they are limited in what they can do to help the athletes through all of the mental and physical developments required just to get them to the Games in a state that gives them the best possible chance of success.

Once the competition starts, the coach is even more limited in what he can do. At the moment of truth, in the heat of the battle, it's the athletes alone who have to deliver. The coaches are sitting in the stands and powerless to help. While that is a reason why coaches should recognise the limits to their influence on the success of an athlete, we should recognise how this incredible lack of control impacts on them. After working so hard, day in, day out, for months or years to help get an athlete to the Games, suddenly there they are in the stands watching their athlete, who's about to compete, unable to have any influence over that final moment that will determine whether all that work will produce success or failure.

All too often, athletes who aren't successful blame their coaches. As a result, most athletes will change coaches several times during their careers. That's not to say that if a coach is not the right coach an athlete should stay with that coach, but it *is* to say that an athlete should look inward for, and take full responsibility for, his own success. If he is not achieving the success that he feels he is capable of, he should assess all the components of his performance and then make the necessary corrections. Instead, the tendency to look outwards first and point the finger has caused many talented athletes to fall short of reaching their full potential.

Contrast that with Chris Hoy, who basically started his career with no coaching at all. Or Daley Thompson, who forged ahead despite a total lack of parental support.

'Why are you playing that game?' Daley's hard-working mother would ask him. 'That's not what we do.' Finally, she laid down the law. 'Either you go to college or you move out,' she told her son.

'I moved out the next day,' Daley recalled. 'I knew I could be the best in the world. I believed in myself, so I left.'

Of course, Daley was proved right. Even so, his mother only ever came to a single one of the Olympic icon's competitions, and that was towards the end of his career. 'Even after I became successful, she never felt that I had a real job,' he said.

TEAM EFFORT

Perhaps working with four different coaches simultaneously, each with his own speciality, filled the parental gap. 'We learned together,' recalled Daley, who to this day remains good friends with all four. 'They learned from me and I learned from them.'

Clearly, however, he did not depend on them to bolster him emotionally or physically. He used his coaches to help him train to his fullest capacity, but as a self-made athlete he didn't need them. Like Chris Hoy, he was already intently barrelling down the path of learning how to perfect his performance. And that, coupled with everything else, made his success almost inevitable.

Although I was as self-motivated as Chris, I also relied on my team, which for several years included training partners in addition to my coach. Training partners are often overlooked but they can be a very important part of an athlete's success. The road to Olympic success is a tough one, and having training partners to lighten the load can help tremendously. Having other athletes sharing all the difficulty, pain and agony of the daily training regimen makes doing what you have to do a lot easier.

Early in my career, I depended on my training partners Tony and Deon, both 400-metre sprinters, to help me get through the daily training. We all worked together each day to make the training easier. In athletics, most training days consist of interval training with the objective of completing intervals in the required time. It takes a lot of energy to run the interval while trying to maintain a particular pace, so Tony, Deon and I would take it in turns to be the lead for the day. That allowed the other two to just run without having to focus on pace.

Having training partners also helps with motivation. There are always days when, as an athlete, you're just not as excited mentally about training, and there are days when you're not feeling as great as you'd like physically. Having training partners to take the lead helps to get you through the training and prevents you from having a sub-standard session.

Simply being around other individuals training at the same time helps too, because it provides an infectious energy and raises everyone's energy level. That's why it's always a good idea for young athletes starting out in their professional career to be in a training environment with a group of more experienced athletes, who can serve as role models, exemplifying the professionalism and commitment required to achieve success at the Olympic level.

During my four years at Baylor and the first four years of my professional career, I always had training partners. Later in my career, after Tony retired from the sport and Deon moved away, I started to train alone. By that time I was at a point where my training was so specialised, and Coach and I were working at such a high level of customised training, that we actually benefited from being the only two at the track. The trade-off was that I no longer had that high-energy environment and had to rely solely on myself to bring the energy to my training sessions. The training was tougher, but by that time I had what it took and could rely on myself alone for the motivation, commitment and dedication required to get through the training effectively.

After the 1998 season Coach and I were approached by Greg Haughton, Jamaica's top 400-metre sprinter, about training with us. Greg had lived in the US since his university days competing for George Mason University. I had known Greg well since he finished third and got the bronze medal in the 1995 World Championships where I took the gold. Coach and I both felt at this point in my career that having another individual training with me would help push me during training sessions, so we welcomed Greg. He turned out to be a great training partner and we both benefited in Sydney, when I won my second Olympic 400-metre gold and Greg took the bronze.

As much as training partners helped me stay the course, like so many other Olympic champions I shared the credit for my wins with Coach. Rebecca Adlington knows just how much of her success she owes to her coach – exactly half. She may be the one racing in the pool, but they're a team. 'I never argue with the work he sets me. He expects me to come in, give him respect and do my work in the pool. I expect him to come in, write up on the board what I'm going to do, and be there for me,' she said. 'Some coaches like to know every single part of their athlete's life. Bill's not really like that. He wants me to be happy and knows I've got to have a life outside swimming. As long as it doesn't affect my swimming in any way, he is happy. If it does start to affect my work in the pool, he will sit down and say, "What's going on?" Apart from that, he's totally focused on the swimming, which is really good. He knows me so well now. He's very good at reading body language. I don't even have to come in and tell him if I'm tired or if there's something wrong; he knows straight away and will pick up on it. He knows exactly when to ease back. He knows how to motivate me, as well. He doesn't get stressed, which is good since I kind of switch off if you start shouting at me. We have such a good relationship because he knows me so well. I've always said I kind of see him like my second dad, if you like. In fact, most people think he *is* my dad.'

I know that feeling. I had the same. Clyde, who is 76 years old now and was my coach from the time I was 18 to the very end of my career, is kind of like another dad. We had such a close relationship that when I came out to the track he knew exactly what I was thinking that day, how I was feeling. Like Rebecca's coach, he knew how to motivate me – and it wasn't by shouting. That didn't work with me either.

Part of the reason I was so successful was that I always expected more out of myself. When I didn't perform at that ever-higher level, I looked first and foremost at myself to determine what I wasn't doing and what I could do better in order to perform better. That process of self-discovery and learning more about myself allowed me to make the adjustments necessary for me to achieve my best.

I do know that today's athletes need to have a sense of responsibility for their talent instilled into them. Nobody else is responsible for that. If you're an athlete, nobody else is going to treat that talent the way that you do. It's not as important to anybody else – not coaches, not parents – as it is to you. Athletes I represent talk to me about their coaches all the time. Often they seem to think the coach isn't doing enough.

'It's not about the coach,' I tell them. 'Look, you've got a small window to achieve your potential here. If you don't, it's over for you. But that coach is still going to be coaching athletes. There's going to be some other athletes he's going to be coaching. I'm going to be representing some other athletes. You're the only one who is going to be left out. So don't rely totally on your coach, don't rely totally on me. We're just your support team. You have take responsibility for yourself and your performance. That means giving the attention and focus needed to achieve your potential.'

CONCLUSION

How do you build an Olympic champion when the road to Olympic success is so difficult and there are so many obstacles and hurdles to overcome? As we've seen, the journey requires natural talent, of course, but also continued development of that talent. That takes a number of personality traits, some which many athletes naturally possess and some that they have developed over the years.

My own quest for Olympic success taught me a great deal about myself and how to achieve success. I thought I could write a manual about that. Writing *this* book, however, has taught me how many more ways there are to reach one's highest potential.

I already knew most of the athletes I interviewed. I certainly knew most of their stories. And yet I learned something new in talking with each one of them about their Olympic success and how they achieved what they did.

I was particularly impressed by Ian Thorpe continuing to believe in himself and never giving up – refusing to give in even just a little bit to the possibility of not competing when the 2000 Games came to his country. He continued to train while injured and even found ways to use the limitations on what he could do as a way to enhance his training.

I knew that Chris Hoy was a great cyclist but had no idea that he started in his sport with no coaching. I was intrigued and blown away, especially when he told me how the IOC eliminated his event and he was forced to take up a new event if he was going to continue his Olympic dream.

Rebecca Adlington telling me about her experiences as a celebrity and suddenly being thrust into the spotlight made me feel sad and angry. But her account of how she handled it made me smile, and I saw the true Olympic champion in her when she talked about resisting pressure and standing proud in the face of the criticism and very hurtful words. Rebecca is also a great example of an athlete knowing herself and exactly what she needs to succeed – in her case by maintaining the consistent simplicity of her training environment.

For years I have discussed and debated sport and life with Daley Thompson. 'That is the Daley Thompson I know,' I first thought when he told me the story of his mother telling him go to college and quit athletics or move out, and it sounded just automatic for him to move out. But after reflecting on this, I'm not sure I would have had the courage to make the same choice at 18.

I was impressed with Usain Bolt's talent when I first saw him compete in the 2003 World Junior Championships as a

CONCLUSION

young 200-metre sprinter. Just like everyone else, I thought his future would be in the 200 metres and 400 metres. I never would have guessed that an athlete with his height could become the fastest man in the world and the greatest 100-metre sprinter in history. Most coaches would have convinced an athlete with his height to focus on the 200 and 400 metres, and most athletes of his height would have never believed that the 100 metres was possible. But Usain believed, and he is now the fastest man in the world. It is that type of belief that makes champions – not belief just because he wanted to run the 100 metres, but belief that he had what it would take and belief that if he improved his start he could compete at 100 metres.

Most champions learned along the way as they gained experience. Most of them became mentally tougher and improved their skills throughout their careers. The athletes I interviewed all got better and better as their careers continued because they learned how to be winners. We all established a habit of winning based on proven successful training, preparation, personal habits and routines. We also learned what works and what doesn't work for us as individual people and athletes.

There are a lot of wrong ways to attempt to achieve success. We all know that. But we often think there is only one right way to achieve success. As the interviews in this book show so clearly, there are many right ways as well. Most champions have figured out what works for them and how they need to train and compete to be the best they can be.

As we saw with Mark Spitz, there are some unorthodox ways to approach being your best. I would not agree with any athlete saying they should not train if they can't get the maximum out of that training. My philosophy was to train every day and wring the most I could out of that training, even if the maximum for that day was less than expected or desired. I still believe, as the stories from so many of the great athletes interviewed for this book show, that every day is an opportunity to get better. Even if it's only a little bit on a particular day, that's better than nothing. I still view a day of missed training as a missed opportunity. But Mark proves that different approaches can be successful.

Finally, I learned that most of these athletes knew themselves better than most people do, and that is what helped them to achieve so much. It is one of the things that I believe was most important in my own success.

The fact that so much work goes into the Olympics for so long makes the experience of winning hard to describe and even harder to achieve. You can't buy it. You can't package it. There's no other way to taste that victory – or even the chance to participate. As Nadia Comaneci said, 'You cannot sign up somebody to be part of an Olympic team. Even if you have a famous dad, you're not going to be part of an Olympic team. It reflects a huge amount of work and dedication to earn that spot. You have to earn it through work, not through connections or anybody else.'

Maybe that's part of what makes winning the Olympics so much more special than any other competition. From 1990 to 1996 I focused on the pure competition, and I did want to beat people by as much as I could. I wanted to cross the finish line so far ahead of everyone else that it was embarrassing for them. That felt good. It felt good to be that much better than everyone else. It wasn't just that I was better. I felt like I had made myself better. I had worked so hard. I felt like I understood how to run my race better than my opponents. The other guys I was running against were talented, but I was able to do more with my talent. That was a high.

The feeling of winning is a great feeling, but it's at a whole other level when it's at the Olympics. At the 1996 Olympics I'd won the 400, but I had to win the 200 to complete the double that I'd gone for so publicly. I'd not only said I was going to do it, the schedule had been changed for me. I was wearing the gold shoes. Anything less than me winning that 200 would have been a failure, at least for me, and I think a lot of other people would have seen it that way as well. The media certainly would have seen it that way.

When I crossed the finish line in the 200 metres, I felt so many different things all at once that I'd never felt before and I've never felt since, even in 2000 when I won.

I was relieved that it was over, because there had been so much pressure. I was relieved that I'd been successful at this monumental task, when so many people had said I would fail. In addition, I'd beaten everybody by so much, and I had run so much faster than the world record, that I was a little shocked. I always thought I could run that fast, but never thought I'd run that fast at the end of eight races, because I was far from fresh.

Finally, having successfully completed the double, I was overjoyed. I hadn't had a chance to celebrate the 400 metres win. My reaction to that gold medal was very subdued because I was already thinking about the 200 race coming up. But once I crossed the finish line in the 200, and could hear the roar of the crowd, which I always blocked out along with everything else during competition, I finally felt like I could celebrate.

Cathy Freeman had a similar experience, and felt a similar sense of relief coupled with joy when she won the gold she was expected to claim for herself and her country at the 2000 Sydney Games. She had watched and been inspired by other Olympic champions. Years of training and races had fostered the belief that she, too, could win Olympic gold. And then she did it. 'When I crossed the line in Sydney, my immediate thought was, "This is what it feels like to be an Olympic champion." I am still trying to work out what happened next, because I suddenly found myself in this really insanely mad place. When I run, I'm in this bubble of silence. It's like I'm in another place. I'm not really with everybody else because I'm so focused. So I didn't hear anybody before the gun went. But as soon as I crossed the line, for the first time I let my guard down and actually joined everybody else in the real world, in that stadium. And I was overwhelmed. Not only has there not been a lot of Australian Olympic track and field achievement, there certainly hasn't been a hell of a lot of Olympic indigenous achievement on the track. What I had accomplished had such big meaning for so many, especially Australians. I felt it in the air that night. Trying to register what I had achieved, I was so overcome that I didn't know what to do but sit down and take my shoes off.'

The Olympics, however, are about more than winning or losing. 'Other than having my kids, competing in the Olympics is the proudest thing I've ever done,' Daley Thompson told me. The uncharacteristically sentimental words didn't stop here. 'There is so much history and the Games have taken place for so long. That's what makes the Games so special.' I'm sure that Daley Thompson could have been one of the greatest footballers had he chosen to pursue that instead of athletics. But I know he has no regrets, because as much as he loved football, it would not have brought him on to the Olympic stage. And I know he would not have missed that experience for anything.

I knew I'd done something special when I won my first two gold medals in 1996. The fact that I had done something that no one had ever done before took the experience of winning at the Olympic level to a whole other level. I was not only a winner twice over, I had made history at the Olympics. I wasn't going to be another name in the Olympic record book, which is special enough. I had set a new Olympic standard for one of history's oldest sports. That's amazing and it gives me a tremendous sense of pride.

It's been 15 years since that accomplishment in 1996, and just a few mornings ago I was on the phone on a conference call and a guy started telling me about how that 200 race was the most special Olympic moment he's ever seen. Strangers come up to me all the time and start recounting the race to me. I'm sitting there thinking, 'Yeah, I know, I was there.' But 15 years after the fact they still remember every aspect of that race and they're still excited about it.

As Sebastian Coe says, the Olympics is the toughest of the competitions. 'It's not a World Championships. It's not Oslo or Zurich. It is such an extraordinary synthesis of the mental and the physical. It probably demands greater will-power and focus than almost anything else. In all our sports it's clearly the pinnacle. We have World Championships, but I think we know the difference. In my sport, we know the difference between the World Championships and an Olympic Games. You've done the most difficult thing you're ever going to be asked to do. Now go off and build on that and learn a little bit more about yourself.

'I've seen it through so many prisms: as an athlete, as a working journalist, as a broadcaster in Australia, and now as a member of the IAAF Council,' Seb told me. 'It is the most complicated piece of project management. You know it. I know it. I went to a Games and I just assumed the village would be there. The bed seemed to have sheets on it. The medals occasionally turned up in the order they were supposed to. The event took place. The transport seemed to be there. When you got back, there was food. If you wanted a massage ... I had no idea what lay behind that.'

I laughed when he said that and countered, 'It's the same thing as people assuming when the gun goes off, you just run the race, and the first person to the finish line wins. It's simple, right?'

His turn to laugh. 'Run fast, turn left,' he said.

CONCLUSION

There is nothing like the Olympic Games, and any athlete fortunate enough to take part understands this. It is such a rare opportunity and one that will become a major part of the rest of your life. I just hope that, whatever the results, the athletes allow that Olympic spirit to infuse them. Jackie Joyner-Kersee's Olympic achievement still gives her pleasure. 'It's really a great feeling when I think back on where I started from and what I was trying to do,' she told me. She knows she gave everything she had inside to her sport, and it changed her life. 'Yesterday I was out to dinner with this young girl who sees me as a role model,' she told me. 'She thinks I'm amazing, but it's amazing what the Olympics do for all of us. It puts us in the history books. It puts us in the lives of people that sometimes we might come in contact with, and sometimes we won't. It's not for me to take that for granted. I embrace it and appreciate it. To know that, wow, I dreamed about this, and it really happened.'

Now she's using her Olympic experience to change the lives of others. 'I am grateful to be able to work with young people, because I can help them to set a solid foundation and put them on the right path.' Although the kids she works with see her as an Olympic hero, she is quick to let them know that she wasn't that promising an athlete when she first started out. 'Being an Olympic athlete, people see you at your highest heights. Especially in the eyes of young people, Olympic success makes you a finished product. For me, it's so important to tell them how to get to that finished product. It's the struggle. It's the commitment to hard work. It's the things that you must do before you can be on television. If that's where you want to go, you've got to do these things when the cameras are not on. The days when people tell you to work hard when no one is watching are so crucial to you going on. If it's an Olympian you want to become, it can happen, but you've got to put the work in now.'

Once the Olympic torch, after its journey around the UK, lights the Olympic cauldron to open the 2012 London Games, some 3.5 billion viewers will tune in to watch 17,000 athletes from more than 200 countries test themselves physically, mentally and emotionally. And as the Games play out over a 15-day span, a whole new set of embryonic Olympic athletes will be born. As Steve Redgrave says, 'The Olympics are magical. It gives kids dreams.'

I couldn't agree more. Kids dream of becoming Olympians, of participating in the Olympics some day like their heroes. But they're not alone. Fans dream of going to the Olympics. Athletes dream of reaching the pinnacle of their sport by making it to the Olympics as competitors. And Olympians dream of becoming Olympic champions. I went through each one of those stages and still wanted to take it further. I was fortunate to do so; after becoming Olympic champion I was able to make Olympic history. And now, since the end of my Olympic career, I work to help other Olympic athletes achieve their dreams. In the process, I get to share their Olympic dream, since I want them to be as fortunate as I was.

Dreams are exactly what make the Olympics so extraordinary. And I know that my Olympic experience allows me

CONCLUSION

to keep dreaming – to keep the flame alive and undimmed. May the upcoming Olympic Games inspire that same torch inside of you.

INDEX

MJ denotes Michael Johnson.

INDEX

INDEX